INTRODUCTION TO FORTRAN IV

INTRODUCTION TO FORTRAN IV

ROBERT H. HAMMOND
Associate Professor of Engineering
Director, Freshman Engineering and Student
Services Division
North Carolina State University

WILLIAM B. ROGERS
Associate Professor of Engineering
Fundamentals
Virginia Polytechnic Institute and
State University

BYARD HOUCK, Jr.
Senior Advisor in Engineering
North Carolina State University

McGRAW-HILL BOOK COMPANY

New York   St. Louis   San Francisco   Auckland   Düsseldorf
Johannesburg Kuala Lumpur   London   Mexico   Montreal   New Delhi
Panama   Paris   São Paulo   Singapore   Sydney   Tokyo   Toronto

INTRODUCTION TO FORTRAN IV

1 2 3 4 5 6 7 8 9   K P K P   7 9 8 7 6 5

Library of Congress Cataloging in Publication Data

Hammond, Robert H
    Introduction to FORTRAN IV.

    Includes index.
      1. FORTRAN (Computer program language) I. Rogers,
William, date joint author. II. Houck, Byard,
joint author. III. Title.
QA76.73.F25H36   001.6'424   75-25763
ISBN 0-07-025895-3

This book was set in Univers by Hemisphere Publishing Corporation.
The editors were B. J. Clark and M. E. Margolies;
the designer was Nicholas Krenitsky;
the production supervisor was Leroy A. Young.
The drawings were done by ECL Art Associates, Inc.
Kingsport Press, Inc., was printer and binder.

CONTENTS

PREFACE

The publication of a new textbook dealing with the FORTRAN computer language might aptly be compared with the arrival of another starling on the horizon to join the flock already roosting in the town park—and greeted with about the same interest and enthusiasm! Professors write textbooks for a variety of reasons: to supplement their salaries; to satisfy a pressing institutional requirement to publish or perish; to impress other professors with their erudition; to gratify their egos; and perhaps once in a great while to help a few less-than-brilliant students to improve their understanding of the rudiments of a specific subject area. The authors plead nolo contendere to any and all of these spurious incentives but sincerely hope that their primary motivation has been to provide a usable textbook which will simplify the fundamentals of FORTRAN for the average college student.

The authors do not claim to be authorities in the field of computer programming or even experts in the use of the FORTRAN language. This brief exposition is not a definitive text, nor is it a comprehensive reference book. In fact, the authors have not even discussed the subject to the extent of their own limited knowledge. The most obvious fault to those real or self-styled experts who take the trouble to critically examine what we have written will be oversimplifications in some areas and significant (by some opinion) omissions in others. To these oversimplifications and omissions, we plead guilty.

Why do we presume to drench an already saturated area with still more verbiage? Because we believe we have said it so the beginning student can understand it. For many years the authors have taught elementary engineering subjects, including FORTRAN programming, to thousands of freshmen at the United States Military Academy, North Carolina State University, and the Virginia Polytechnic Institute and State University. At the same time, we have taught many novice professors the techniques of classroom presentation and have supervised their subsequent performance. If there is any field in which the authors may modestly claim expertise, it is in the forced-feeding of required technical foundation subject matter to large numbers of generally indifferent beginners.

It is for this mass audience of indifferent beginners that this textbook is written. The authors have attempted to reduce the often mysterious and seemingly complex world of the computer to its simplest elements. The terminology has been purged of unnecessary "computerese." Both the language and the mathematics should be readily understood by anyone with a reasonable high school education and average verbal comprehension.

No attempt has been made to present everything there is to know about FORTRAN. Enough is covered to permit the student to understand the fundamental techniques of the language and, with practice, to write meaningful programs. In general, only one way of accomplishing a desired result is discussed. Options, exceptions, shortcuts, and exotic statements or routines not likely to be encountered by the beginner have been avoided. The text material has been implemented by illustrations which provide a brief graphic summary of fundamental instructions. Flow diagrams and computer printouts illustrate applications and the results obtained from each routine discussed. Illustrative problems previously introduced are again used in succeeding chapters so that the student can concentrate on the new FORTRAN instruction being discussed without also worrying about the concepts in a new problem. The problems given at the end of the various chapters are basic in concepts so that the student can concentrate on applying the FORTRAN principles and not be overcome by the concepts involved in the problem. When a student has demonstrated an understanding of FORTRAN, the teacher may assign more advanced problems that involve the teacher's interests and objectives.

This textbook is written primarily for students at institutions where the WATFIV compiler for FORTRAN IV is used. There are a few discussions that apply only to WATFIV users. However if WATFIV is not the compiler used, the teacher can eliminate those discussions and adapt the other discussions to fit other compilers.

The authors have enjoyed some success in their classes with this material in the form of handouts, projecturals, and chalkboard sketches. We now offer it to you, the average beginning student, with the hope that it will ease somewhat the process of learning this fascinating FORTRAN.

And, to you, professor: There should be sufficient material in this textbook to keep both you and your students gainfully occupied for one full semester. Or, if you talk fast, it can be covered in one quarter.

Robert H. Hammond
William B. Rogers
Byard Houck, Jr.

INTRODUCTION TO
FORTRAN IV

WHAT IS A 1. DIGITAL COMPUTER?

INTRODUCTION

There are two types of computers in wide use today: digital and analog computers. The digital computer is essentially a counting device and operates with numbers represented by a finite sequence of digits. The analog computer operates by measuring the magnitudes of the quantities in an electric circuit which is set up to parallel (or be analogous to) the equation of the phenomenon being investigated. Analog-computer results are usually displayed as a curve on a cathode-ray tube, and numerical quantities are not shown.

The needs of modern-day computations have led to the increasing use of a combination of digital and analog computers. This combination is known as a *hybrid computer*. A detailed discussion of the use of hybrid computers, as well as any discussion of analog computers, is outside the scope of this text, but all students should be aware of their existence.

1-2

THE BASIC COMPONENTS OF DIGITAL COMPUTERS

A general-purpose digital computer consists basically of five components or functional units: input, storage, arithmetic, control, and output units. The relationship of these functional units is represented by the block diagram in Fig. 1-1. Information is interchanged between these units as indicated by the arrows.

a The Input Unit The *input unit* places the desired instructions and data into the storage unit. A commonly used input device is the *card reader*, illustrated in Fig. 1-2. A card reader senses the holes punched in a computer card and transmits the information punched in the cards to the storage unit. This is the

1

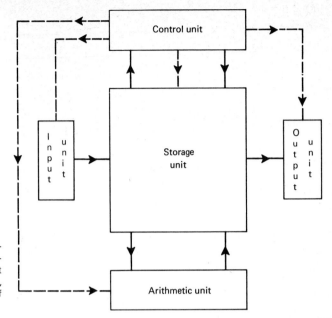

FIG. 1-1
Basic components, or functional units, of a digital computer. Solid lines represent
flow of information (data),
dashed lines represent flow of
control signals.

FIG. 1-2
IBM 3505 card reader. (*Courtesy of IBM.*)

only input device that will be discussed in this text. However, other input
devices that may be available include the typewriter, the tape drive, and
punched paper tape.

Before using the card reader, blank computer cards must first be punched

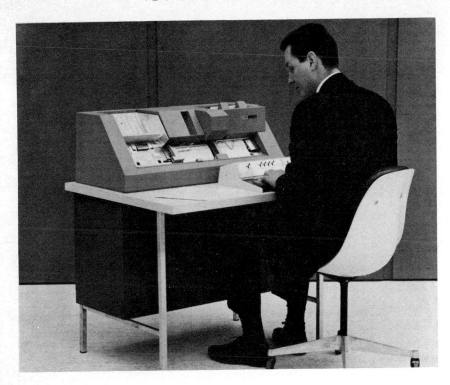

FIG. 1-3
IBM 029 card punch. (*Courtesy of IBM.*)

on a machine called a *card punch*, illustrated in Fig. 1-3. Brief instructions covering the basic operation of the IBM 029 card punch are given in Appendix B. The keys of the card punch are similar to the keys of a standard typewriter; however, pressing them causes one or more holes to be punched in the card. The rectangular hole or pattern of holes represents the desired character. Unfortunately, several models of card punches are in use which, in some cases, cut different hole patterns for the same character. This causes problems, particularly when using cards punched at another computer center. Students should always check to ensure that the cards are punched or have been punched by a card punch compatible with their systems.

b The Storage Unit The *storage unit* consists of many *core planes* (see Fig. 1-4). Each core plane is made up of a number of ferrite cores (or rings) strung on hair-thin wires. Dependent upon how current is passed through these wires, each ring can be magnetized with either a clockwise or a counterclockwise magnetic field. The rings are divided into groups of rings, with each group known as a "word." Each word has its own unique address which the computer knows. The size of a word can vary from a 1- to 1Ø-digit number (or more), depending upon the capability of the individual computer. Computer users must always determine the word size of the particular computer that they will be using.

A distinctive feature of the storage unit of a general-purpose computer is destructive *read-in* and nondestructive *read-out*. Each time information is stored

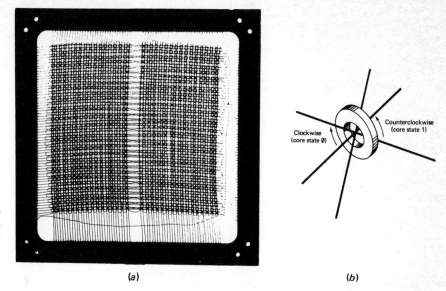

(a)

(b)

FIG. 1-4
(a) Core Plane with ferrite cores visible on intersecting conductors (*courtesy of IBM*); (b) enlarged drawing of a core.

in a given word, the previous contents of that word are erased as the new data are read in. However, the contents of that word can be moved to another word with a different address without changing the contents of the original word. This feature is important to remember in preparing instructions for the computer. A second characteristic of this type of storage unit is called *random access*, which means that any word address in the storage unit is as easy to find as any other address and takes the same amount of time.

Auxiliary storage capacity may be added by using magnetic tapes or discs. Access to information stored on tape is sequential. To retrieve a given item, the entire tape must be examined from some starting point to the location of the desired information. Thus, it may take more time to find one word than another. The magnetic disc is a cross between random and sequential access and requires less time to search than the tape. The discussion in this text will be confined to the basic random-access storage unit. When students advance to the point where auxiliary storage capacity is required for their programs, they should consult the experts at a computer center or refer to a more comprehensive computer textbook.

The storage unit is also known as the *memory unit*. The term *memory* is not used in this text because it implies the human capability to remember. To those unfamiliar with the computer, it also implies the ability to think. Both these implications are misleading. A computer does not remember, nor does it think for itself. The computer does precisely what it is instructed to do—nothing more, nothing less. The computer's sequence of actions and the results thereof depend solely upon the instructions it receives from a human programmer. An often used expression among computer people is "garbage in—garbage out," which means that unless the logic of the program is correctly planned to perform the desired calculations, the output will be meaningless or misleading.

FIG. 1-5
IBM 3211 line printer. (*Courtesy of IBM.*)

c The Arithmetic Unit The *arithmetic unit* is a portion of the computer set aside for performing the basic arithmetic operations: addition, subtraction, multiplication, and division. It also provides temporary storage for holding the results of these operations. This small storage unit is known as the *accumulator*.

d The Control Unit The *control unit* is the heart of the modern digital computer. It selects an instruction and causes the computer to obey that instruction whether it be to read a data card, perform some arithmetic operation, compare two values, or print results. The control unit consists primarily of two parts: a small storage unit known as the *instruction register* (IR) and a device called the *instruction counter* (IC).

e The Output Unit Printed results from the computer may be obtained from the *printer*. This machine prints the pages of results commonly associated with computer systems and is illustrated in Fig. 1-5. Other output units punch cards, store information on magnetic or punched paper tape, utilize the typewriter on the computer console or remote terminal, or display results on a cathode-ray tube (CRT).

1-3

THE STORED-PROGRAM CONCEPT

Before any problem can be solved on the computer, a set of step-by-step instructions must be written which define precisely how to solve the problem. This set of instructions is called a *program*. The program must be written in a *language* which the computer can understand. Each step of the program is called a *statement*. Usually each statement is punched on a separate card called an *instruction card*. After all instruction cards have been punched and arranged in order, each item of numerical data is punched on a card. These cards are called *data cards* and follow the last instruction card. Dependent upon how the program is written, each item of data may be punched on a seperate card or many items of data may be punched on the same card.

In the preceding paragraph we stated that the program must be written in a language which the computer can understand. Actually, the computer can understand only *machine language*, a language which is complex and lengthy. The computer cannot understand directly the user-oriented FORTRAN language. Instead an intermediate program must be employed which can be stored in the computer and translate the user-oriented FORTRAN into the machine-oriented language of the computer. Such a program is called a *compiler*. Most compilers also include diagnostic routines which result in printing error messages that point out certain standard programming errors for the programmer's assistance. This capability will be discussed in more detail in Chap. 9. Another usual output of the compiler is a listing of the exact FORTRAN program read by the computer so that the programmer can see in printed form what was actually contained on the punched cards. The compiler program used for the programs illustrated in this text is known as WATFIV.

The computer solution to a particular problem is separated into two phases. First, the entire set of instructions (or program) is read, translated, and filed in the storage unit, each individual instruction occupying a word (or words as required) with a distinct address; this first phase—reading the program, translating, and filing it in the storage unit—is called *compilation*. Second, each separate instruction is called sequentially from the storage unit and held temporarily in the instruction register of the control unit while that instruction is executed; This second phase—performing the operation called for in the instruction—is called *execution*. This two-phase procedure in which the computer first stores the program in its entirety (compilation) and then automatically and sequentially follows those instructions is known as the *stored-program concept* and is the essence of digital-computer operation.

Consider a simple arithmetic problem: the sum of two numbers such as 32 + 18 = 5∅. Without attempting to simulate any actual computer language but using instructions understandable to the reader and assuming computer acceptability, the following *program* has been written to read two numerical values, 32 and 18, punched on two data cards and to compute and print the sum. (Each instruction is assumed to have been punched on an individual instruction card and identified alphabetically by letters A, B, C, etc. The numerical values 32 and 18 have each been punched on a separate data card.)

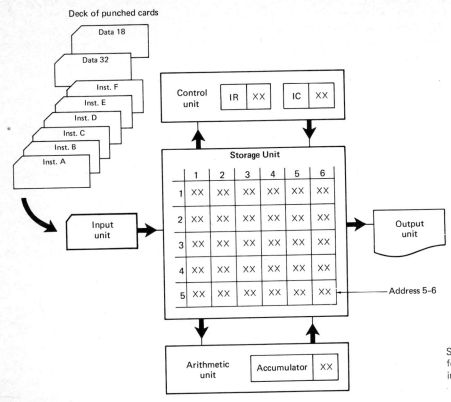

FIG. 1-6*a*
Simulation of computer ready
for input of instructions. IR,
instruction register; IC, instruction counter.

Instruction A: Read a data card and store its value in address 2-1

Instruction B: Read the next data card and store its value in address 2-2

Instruction C: Copy the value in address 2-1 into the accumulator

Instruction D: Add the value in address 2-2 to the value in the accumulator

Instruction E: Store the value in the accumulator in address 2-3

Instruction F: Print the value in address 2-3

(End of Instructions)

Data: 32

Data: 18

Figure 1-6 represents a graphical simulation of the five functional units of
the computer as described in Sec. 1-2. The storage unit provides for 3Ø
"words" whose locations are specified by a two-digit numerical "address"
identifying the row and column, respectively. (For example, the address of the
bottom right space or word is 5-6, row 5, column 6.) The XX's in the storage
unit, the instruction register (IR), instruction counter (IC), and the accumulator (Fig. 1-6*a*) represent miscellaneous information remaining in storage after

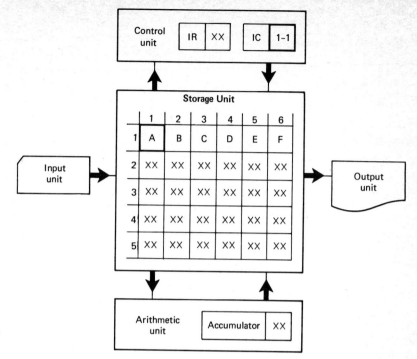

FIG. 1-6*b*
Simulation of computer ready
for execution.

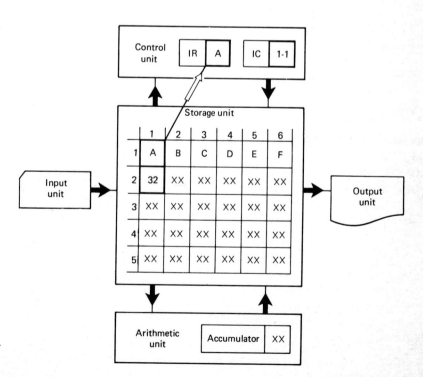

FIG. 1-6*c*
Simulation of computer after
execution of instruction A.

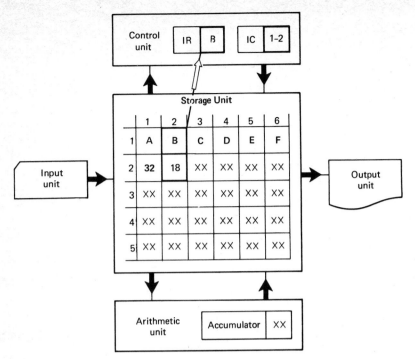

FIG. 1-6*d*
Simulation of computer after
execution of instruction B.

completion of the previous program. When current information is read into storage, previously stored information will be destroyed. To start the sequence, the card deck is placed in the card reader (as indicated in Fig. 1-6*a*), the "start" button is pressed, and action begins.

The condition of the computer after all instructions have been read in (compilation is complete) is shown in Fig. 1-6*b*. Instructions A, B, C, D, E, and F are stored sequentially in words with addresses 1-1, 1-2, 1-3, 1-4, 1-5, and 1-6, respectively. The information remaining from previous calculations (XX) has been destroyed in addresses 1-1 to 1-6 and replaced by the new and relevant information. Note that the instruction counter (IC) has been automatically set to the address of the first instruction (1-1). Execution of the program begins.

In Fig. 1-6*c*, the first instruction (instruction A in address 1-1) has been "copied" into the instruction register (IR), destroying the previous instruction (XX) but leaving instruction A unchanged in address 1-1. The computer then executes instruction A:

Read a data card and store its value in address 2-1.

The first data card in sequence is read, and the numerical value punched therein (32) is stored in word address 2-1. The IC automatically increments to the next address in sequence (1-2).

Figure 1-6*d* illustrates the execution of instruction B. The IC calls for the instruction in address 1-2 (instruction B) to be copied into the IR destroying

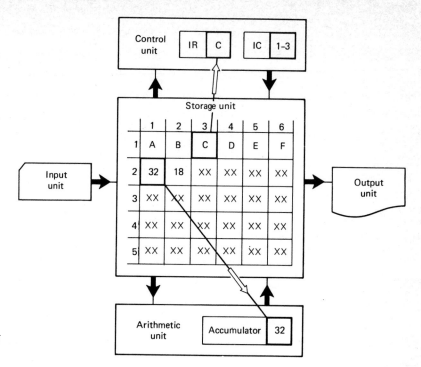

FIG. 1-6*e*
Simulation of computer after
execution of instruction C.

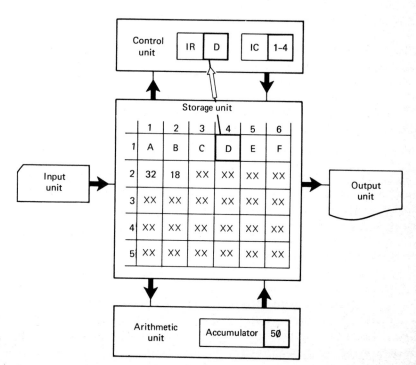

FIG. 1-6*f*
Simulation of computer after
execution of instruction D.

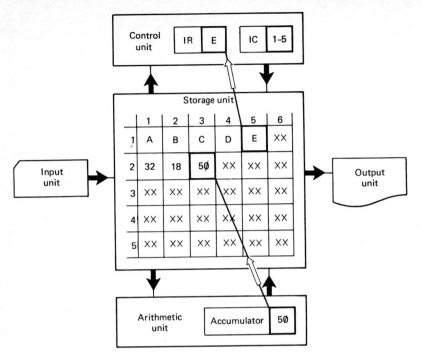

FIG. 1-6*g*
Simulation of computer after
execution of instruction E.

the previous instruction (instruction A). Note that instruction B remains unchanged in address 1-2. The computer then executes instruction B:

Read a data card and store its value in address 2-2.

The next data card in sequence is read, and the numerical value punched therein (18) is stored in word address 2-2. The IC automatically increments to the next address in sequence (1-3).

In Fig. 1-6*e*, the instruction in address 1-3 (instruction C) has been copied to the IR. Instruction C is executed:

Copy the value in address 2-1 into the accumulator.

The value in address 2-1 (32) is copied into the accumulator (ACC) where arithmetic operations are performed. The previous value in the ACC (XX) has been erased. The IC now increments to 1-4.

The instruction in address 1-4 (instruction D) is copied into the IR (Fig. 1.6*f*). Instruction D is executed:

Add the value in address 2-2 to the value in the accumulator.

The value in address 2-2 (18) is added to the value in the ACC (32). The sum (5Ø) replaces the previous value (32) in the ACC. The IC increments to 1-5.

The instruction in address 1-5 (instruction E) is copied into the IR (Fig. 1-6*g*). Instruction E is executed:

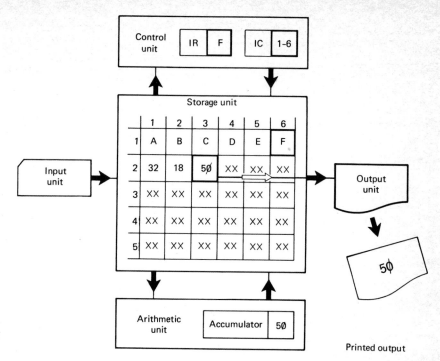

FIG. 1-6*h*
Simulation of computer after execution of instruction F.

Store the value in the accumulator in address 2-3.

The value in the ACC (5Ø) is copied into word address 2-3. The IC increments to 1-6.

Finally, as illustrated in Fig. 1-6*h*, the last instruction in address 1-6 (instruction F) is copied into the IR. Instruction F is executed:

Print the value in address 2-3.

The value in address 2-3 (5Ø) is transmitted to the output unit, and the result of the computation (5Ø) is printed on a sheet of paper.

The preceding description is an oversimplified simulation of the operational sequence of a digital computer. The first computers developed could accept only one hand-fed instruction at a time, a slow process indeed. However, with the development of the stored-program concept and its related increase in speed, the use of the digital computer has grown rapidly and has been extended to many fields of endeavor.

Succeeding chapters will discuss the preparation of computer instructions needed to solve a wide variety of numerical problems. No further direct reference will be made to the simplified explanation presented in this chapter. However, an awareness of the stored-program concept will reduce the potential for errors in logic in future computer programming.

Binary Digits			Decimal Value
$2^2 = 4$	$2^1 = 2$	$2^0 = 1$	
Ø	Ø	Ø	Ø
Ø	Ø	1	1
Ø	1	Ø	2
Ø	1	1	3
1	Ø	Ø	4
1	Ø	1	5
1	1	Ø	6
1	1	1	7

Example:
The decimal value 5 is represented in the binary system by 1Ø1. (1 four + Ø twos + 1 one.) In the digital computer, the binary digits 1Ø1 can be stored by three ferrite cores—the first magnetized with a counterclockwise field representing core state 1, the second magnetized with a clockwise field representing core state Ø, and the third again magnetized with a counterclockwise field representing core state 1.

FIG. 1-7
Binary numbers and the computer.

1-4
HOW NUMBERS ARE STORED

Since all numbers used by the computer are stored in the storage unit employing groups, or "words," of ferrite rings (refer to Fig. 1-4), the problem arises as to how to store numbers. As there are only two conditions of these ferrite rings that can be recognized, it is obvious that it would be difficult to represent the 1Ø different digits of the common decimal system. Therefore, the binary number system is used to represent, or store, numbers.

The binary number system can define numbers by expressing them as different powers of 2. Assume that when a ring is magnetized with a counterclockwise field, the presence of a particular power of 2 is indicated (core state 1); when a ring is magnetized with a clockwise field, the absence of that power of 2 is indicated (core state Ø). Thus, only two conditions are required, and the storage unit can be employed to represent the numbers used. Figure 1-7 describes how a group of three ferrite rings (a "word") can be used to represent the decimal digits from Ø to 7.

It is not necessary that the beginning programmer thoroughly understand the binary number system. It is important only to know that the binary

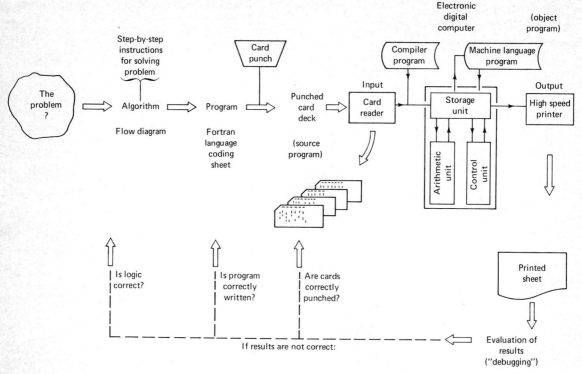

FIG. 1-8
The "big picture." Diagram of a digital computer solution from problem recognition to printed results.

system is used by the computer and that, consequently, only exact powers of 2 can be stored precisely. All other numbers (not exact powers of 2) are very close approximations of their actual decimal values. This fact, which has an important bearing on the accuracy of computer results, will be discussed in greater detail in Chap. 11.

1-5
THE BIG PICTURE

The preceding sections have discussed, in some detail, the components of digital computers, how a program can be translated and placed in the storage unit, and how the computer then executes the program. The remaining chapters will describe how the user-oriented computer language FORTRAN IV can be employed in preparing the computer program. But, first, a brief description of the total procedure will help the student understand the "big picture" of computer usage.

The first step, as shown in Fig. 1-8, is to recognize that a problem exists and that its complexity calls for a computer solution. Then the solution algorithm is prepared. An *algorithm* is defined as a rule of procedure for solving a mathematical problem that frequently involves repetition of an operation. Actually, an algorithm consists of a series of step-by-step instructions for solving the problem. It is most often presented in a graphical form known as a *flow diagram* (Chap. 5).

These step-by-step instructions are then written in a user-oriented computer language (Chaps. 2, 3, 4, 6, 7, and 10) which is then punched onto computer cards. The program is known as the *source program.* The cards are then fed into a card reader, which translates the holes punched in the cards into an electrical form that the computer can utilize. After reading, the cards are returned to the user, as indicated in Fig. 1-8, for future use if required.

As the cards are being read, the instructions of the source program are translated by the compiler program into a machine-language program that the computer can understand and perform. This form of the program is known as the *object program* and is stored in the storage unit.

When the object program is completed, the control unit takes over and the required solution is performed, with the results usually printed on a sheet of paper. These results must be carefully evaluated (Chap. 9) to ascertain whether or not they are correct and/or as expected. If errors or inaccuracies occur, the steps leading to the computer must be carefully studied for any possible errors of logic or punching.

HOW DOES THE 2. COMPUTER COMPUTE?

2-1
INTRODUCTION

In Chap. 1 it was pointed out that instructions and numbers are stored in addressable locations within the storage unit of the computer. The purpose of this chapter is to discuss the various types of constants and variables, how arithmetic operations are expressed, and how calculations are defined and stored. The language used as the basis for this and succeeding chapters is FORTRAN IV, an abbreviation for the fourth generation of a computer language known as FORmula TRANslation.

Beginning students are often confused by such terms as machine language, processor, object program, and source program. A complete understanding of these terms is not necessary for students to start preparing a sequence of instructions (program) that will enable them to use the computer to solve a particular problem. Students must know only that within the facilities available to the personnel of a computer center there exists a voluminous set of detailed machine-language instructions that enables the computer to execute the series of simplified instructions that students prepare under the rules of FORTRAN IV.

2-2
THE FORTRAN CHARACTER SET

The FORTRAN language utilizes the following alphabetic, numeric, and special characters of the English language and mathematics:

1 The 26 alphabetic characters of the English language: A to Z

2 The 1Ø decimal digits: Ø to 9

3 Special characters, the most common of which are

+ plus	. period (decimal point)
− minus	, comma
* asterisk	' apostrophe
/ slash	(left parenthesis
= equals sign (or assignment symbol)	) right parenthesis

These characters are combined to form words, numbers, and expressions that are readily understandable to a programmer and that are used to compose FORTRAN *statements.* A FORTRAN statement is an explicit instruction to the computer to perform a single simple operation, for example, read a value punched in a card, perform a mathematical operation, repeat a series of operations, or print the results of a calculation.

A FORTRAN *program* consists of a series of these step-by-step instructions, or statements. FORTRAN statements are of various types, and those used most frequently will be discussed in detail at the appropriate time in this text.

2-3
FORTRAN NUMBERS (CONSTANTS)

A number is a series of numerical digits with or without a decimal point and with or without an algebraic sign. The maximum- and minimum-size number that can be used varies from computer to computer. Students should determine the size (range) of numbers that can be handled by a particular computer. Numbers used in FORTRAN are in one of two forms: integer numbers or real numbers.

a Integer Numbers An *integer number* (Fig. 2-1) is literally an integer, i.e., a whole number without a decimal point. It may be zero or any positive or negative value. As stated previously, the number of digits that can be used depends upon the capacity of the computer. In general, it can be said that an integer number must be less than about ten digits. Decimal points are not permitted in integer values. The value 123 is an integer value, but the value 123. is not an integer value. Although integer numbers must be written without a decimal point so that the computer can identify them as integers, the computer will assume a decimal point immediately following the rightmost digit.

Certain peculiarities result from integer arithmetic operations. The computer is programmed so that the results of arithmetic operations with integer numbers must also be integers. Consider the operation 4 ÷ 5. The arithmetic result is 0.8, a fractional value; but the computer will not accept the fractional result. Instead, the computer will drop the decimal part and assign the integer 0 as the result. Ignoring this condition of FORTRAN can cause significant errors in final results. Integer numbers should be avoided in computations, except when used as exponents. Normally integer numbers are used

---

Integer Numbers

No decimal point.

No fractional values.

Used as counters and exponents.

Results of integer arithmetic are rounded to next *lower* integer.

Remainders resulting from division are lost (truncated).

N = 4/3	value of N is 1
J = 8/5	value of J is 1
K = 17/5	value of K is 3

FIG. 2-1
Integer numbers.

for counters and identification numbers and in similar operations where fractional values are not likely to occur.

b Real Numbers Most numbers used in FORTRAN arithmetic operations are decimal numbers called *real numbers* (Fig. 2-2). There are two forms in which real numbers can be expressed: with an exponent and without an exponent. The value 123. is a real number without an exponent. The decimal point following the last digit identifies it to the computer as a real number. A zero following the decimal point is not required but may be used.

A real number with an exponent is expressed as a decimal number between Ø.1 and 1.Ø times a power of 1Ø. For example, the real number 123. can be expressed as $Ø.123 \times 10^3$. Written for the computer, this number becomes Ø.123E3. The E3 means that the exponent, or power of 1Ø, is 3. Therefore, since 10^3 is 1ØØØ, the value Ø.123E3 is the same as Ø.123 times 1ØØØ (or 123.).

Within the computer all real numbers are expressed in exponential form. Consider the operation Ø.123E3 × Ø.53E2. Putting these values in the more

---

Real Numbers

Used in most computations.

Decimal point *must* be written.

A = 4./3.	value of A is 1.333 (and so on)
B = 8./5.	value of B is 1.6
X = 17./5.	value of X is 3.4
Y = Ø.5E2/Ø.2E1	value of Y is 25.Ø

FIG. 2-2
Real numbers.

usual form, we have 123. X 53., and 6519. is the result. However, the computer stores the result in exponential form (Ø.6519E4). In other words, within the computer the results of operations involving real numbers are always expressed as a decimal number between Ø.1 and 1.Ø with the power of 1Ø exponent adjusted to reflect the true decimal value.

c Mixed Mode The term *mixed mode* refers to expressions containing both integer (mode) and real (mode) numbers. Except for a few specific exceptions, mixing of modes can lead to trouble. Some computers will not accept mixed-mode expressions and will reject the program. Other computers will transform the integer numbers of the operation to a real value and proceed, resulting at times in unexpected answers. For the beginner, the safest procedure is to always avoid mixed-mode expressions. The specific exceptions mentioned previously will be discussed later.

2-4
FORTRAN VARIABLE NAMES (VARIABLES)

A quantity that is given a name and varies in value during calculations or is originally of unknown value is called a *variable.* The value assigned to a variable may be either integer or real. A variable name may consist of from one to six letters or letters and digits, depending upon the computer used. Some computers limit the size of the variable name to five characters. However, for all computers, the first character of the variable name must be a letter of the alphabet.

a Integer Variables When a variable is to be assigned integer values, the first character of the name must be I, J, K, L, M, or N—the integer designators. After the first letter, succeeding characters may be any letter or digit. Examples of acceptable integer variable names are I, J2, and NUMBER. Examples of unacceptable integer variable names are X (first character not an integer designator), 2K (first character not a letter), and INTEGER (too many characters).

b Real Variables When a variable is to be assigned real values, the first character may be any letter of the alphabet other than those reserved for the first letter of integer variables. As with integer variables, the number of characters may vary from one to six, and after the first letter, succeeding characters may be any letter or digit. Examples of acceptable real variable names are ALPHA, BIG, YCUBED, PART2, and X. Examples of unacceptable real variable names are 2XRAY (first character not a letter), KAPPA (first letter makes it an integer variable), and X/Y (contains a character other than a letter or digit). Figure 2-3 summarizes the rules for determining variable names.

2-5
FORTRAN ARITHMETIC OPERATIONS

FORTRAN provides for five basic arithmetic operations: addition, subtraction,

Integer-Variable Designators:	I	J	K	L	M	N

Real-Variable Designators: All other letters A to H; O to Z.

Rules for variable names

1. First character *must* be a letter.

2. Subsequent characters may be any combination of letters and digits. Special characters *may not* be used.

3. Variable name *must not exceed six* characters (for most computers).

4. Integer variables *must* begin with I, J. K, L, M, or N only.

5. Real variables *must* begin with any other letter, A to H or O to Z.

6. Blank spaces may be inserted to improve readability. Blank spaces do not count as one of the six allowable characters.

7. The same name must not be used for more than one variable in a given program.

8. Before a variable name can be used in computation, *it must be assigned a numerical value by either* an arithmetic statement or a READ statement.

Integer-variable names			Real-variable names		
NUMBER,	NUM,	N	RADIUS,	RAD,	R
MONTH,	MO,	M	AREA,	AR,	A
ITEM,	JOHN,	I, J	CIRCUM,	CIR,	C
NUM 2	ITEM 3		R1,	R2,	R3

FIG. 2-3
Variable names.

multiplication, division, and exponentiation (raising a number to a power). Each operation is represented by an easily distinguishable symbol:

Addition   +

Subtraction   −

Multiplication   *

Division   /

Exponentiation   **

All these symbols can be found on a standard typewriter. The symbols for addition (+) and subtraction (−) are the same as those customarily used. The usual symbols for multiplication are X or ·; however, X might be mistaken for the letter X, and · is not available on the standard typewriter. In FORTRAN there can be no double meanings for any symbol and all symbols must be available on the typewriter; therefore, the asterisk (*) is used as the symbol for multiplication. The (/) has long been used as a division symbol, particularly when writing arithmetic operations on a single line, as must be done in FORTRAN. The standard representation for raising a number to a power is X^a, where a is the power to which X is to be raised. Since all FORTRAN operations must be written on one line, the double asterisk symbol (**) is used to represent exponentiation. The double asterisk is considered as one symbol, so that there is no confusion between it and the symbol for multiplication.

An important rule to remember in FORTRAN is that no two symbols of operation may be written side by side. Doing so will result in the program being rejected by the computer. In some cases where the minus sign is used, it may be necessary to rearrange the symbols of the expression to avoid adjacent symbols of operation. For example, X/−Y may be rewritten as X/(−Y) or −X/Y without changing the meaning or value of the expression. Note the use of parentheses to separate the two symbols of operation.

2-6
FORTRAN EXPRESSIONS

A FORTRAN expression describes the mathematical relationship of a group of constants and/or variables. In some cases, an expression may consist of a single constant, variable, or function (to be described in Chap. 6). X, X*Y, X**2, and (X+1.)+(Y−1.) are examples of FORTRAN expressions. More often, several of these elements are combined by using arithmetic symbols of operation and/or parentheses. In evaluating a FORTRAN expression, the computer follows a strictly ordered sequence or hierarchy of operations:

1 Clear parentheses: scanning from left to right, clearing from inside out

2 Exponentiation: scanning from left to right, exponentiating from *right* to *left*

3 Multiplication and/or division: scanning and multiplying or dividing, as required, from left to right

4 Addition and/or subtraction: scanning and adding or subtracting, as required, from left to right

When a FORTRAN expression is to be evaluated, the computer must first scan the entire expression for parentheses, proceeding from left to right. Parentheses are cleared inside out from left to right. The expression is scanned again to see if any exponentiation is indicated. If so, the exponentiation is performed from *right* to *left*. Next the expression is scanned to see if any multiplication and/or division is required. If so, those operations are done from left to right. Finally, the expression is scanned and all addition and/or subtraction is done, again proceeding from left to right. The result is a single value which is the value of the expression.

Before discussing what is done with that single value, let us examine some simple expressions to show why it is important to understand the hierarchy of operations. First consider the expression A*B**2. Since there are no parentheses to be cleared, the first computer operation is exponentiation to calculate the square of B. If we represent the resulting value of this operation by BB, the expression becomes A*BB. Next the value A is multiplied by the value BB. The result is the value of the expression.

Another expression could be C+D/E. The computer will first scan the expression for parentheses and exponentiation. Since neither exists, the computer will look for multiplication and/or division and divide D by E; then add to C the result of that calculation. The sum is the value of the expression.

Suppose, however, that in the first expression it was desired to square the product of A times B, and that in the second expression the desired result was the sum of C and D divided by E? As written, these results could not be calculated because the computer must evaluate each expression in the order described. However, the desired results can be attained through the use of parentheses. The computer is instructed to first scan all expressions for parentheses before doing any calculations. When it finds a left parenthesis, it looks for the next right parenthesis and then performs all calculations within the parentheses as described previously. Therefore, if the first expression is written (A*B)**2, the result will be the square of the product of A and B; if the second expression is written (C+D)/E, the result will be the sum of C and D divided by E.

Consider a more complex expression A*(B+C/(D**2)). In determining the value of this expression, the computer first scans for parentheses. Finding a left parenthesis just before B, it then looks for a closing (right) parenthesis. But as it scans from left to right, the computer finds another left parenthesis just before D. It will then ignore the previous left parenthesis and continue looking for a right parenthesis, finding it just after the 2. The computer then evaluates between the parentheses and determines the square of D. It scans for parentheses again, as before, and, finding a match, will evaluate within the parentheses by dividing C by the square of D and then adding the result to B. Representing the result of these calculations by EE, the expression becomes A*EE. The computer looks for parentheses again and, finding none, will evaluate the expression by multiplying the value of A by the value of EE.

The preceding explanation emphasizes an important rule of FORTRAN: In any expression, *there must be as many left-parenthesis characters as there are right and vice versa.* If the parentheses are unbalanced, the computer will reject the program. The programmer must carefully examine every expression to ensure that the calculations to be performed by the computer are exactly as intended. If parentheses are used, nested parentheses (parentheses within parentheses) must be balanced. Figure 2-4 shows a summation of the basic rules governing FORTRAN arithmetic operations and expressions.

Arithmetic Operations

Operation	Math Notation	FORTRAN Symbol	FORTRAN Expression
Addition	$A + B$	+	A+B
Subraction	$C - B$	−	C−B
Multiplication	$A \times B$	*	A*B
Division	$A \div B$	/	A/B
Exponentiation	R^2	**	R**2

Arithmetic Expressions

Math	FORTRAN Expression
$3.1416R$	3.1416*R
πr^2	3.1416*R**2
$\dfrac{\pi d^2}{4}$	(3.1416*D**2)/4.
$(A + B)^3$	(A+B)**3
$\sqrt{a^2 + b^2}$	(A**2+B**2)**.5

Expressions must be either *integer* mode or *real* mode. *Mixed modes are not allowed.*

Exceptions: An integer exponent may be used with real numbers or variable names.

$\left.\begin{array}{l} \text{X**2} \\ \text{6.0**2} \end{array}\right\}$ (Correct)

I**2. (Not Correct)

No two operators may appear in sequence:

A/−B must be written A/(−B) or −A/B

2-7
ARITHMETIC ASSIGNMENT STATEMENTS

A FORTRAN program consists of a series of step-by-step instructions called *statements*. Statements of different types accomplish various results. Numerical computations are accomplished through the arithmetic assignment statement. An *arithmetic assignment statement* assigns the result of arithmetic computations (the numerical value of an arithmetic expression) to a named variable in a specific storage location. For example, consider

Y=A∗B∗∗2

This statement tells the computer to evaluate the expression to the right of the = character and to assign that value to the variable named Y and file it somewhere in storage. This is one of the beauties of FORTRAN! The programmer does not have to specify storage locations and remember where they are. The computer itself will assign a storage location to any variable name to the left of the = character the first time that name is used, and if that variable is used in subsequent calculations, the computer will know where the variable has been stored and automatically fetch it when required.

This brings out another important rule of FORTRAN: *There can be only one variable name to the left of the = character (assignment symbol).* Violations of this rule will result in rejection of the program by the computer.

The student should note that we have carefully refrained from calling the = character an *equals sign*. In FORTRAN the symbol = is not used to indicate mathematical equality but is strictly an *assignment symbol*. It tells the computer to assign the value of the expression to the right of the symbol to the variable to the left of the symbol. For this reason, the statement X=X+1. is a perfectly correct arithmetic assignment statement. It tells the computer to fetch the value previously assigned to X, add the value 1 to X, and then file the new value in the storage location designated for X. This feature enables the programmer to increment (or sequentially change) the numerical value assigned to a given variable name.

The arithmetic assignment statement may also be used to assign the value of a constant to a unique variable name; PI=3.14159 is an example. Here the constant 3.14159 is to be used in subsequent calculations. This statement means that the constant is stored in some location known as PI and when the constant is subsequently used in an expression, it can be called simply by using PI instead of the longer numerical value.

There are times when it is desired to *truncate* (drop the fractional part of) a real value, or, in other words, to change a real value to an integer value. An example is the statement I=Y. Here the real value Y is changed to integer form by truncating, or dropping off, all decimal portions. However, if the value assigned to Y is 6.6, the resulting value assigned to I will be 6, which is not the nearest value to 6.6. If the statement is changed to I=Y+0.5, the result will be the assignment of the value 7 to the variable I. Thus, *rounding* rather than truncation has been accomplished. If the decimal portion of Y is less than 0.5, it will still be dropped. If the decimal portion of Y is exactly 0.5 or greater than 0.5, the resulting value assigned to I will be raised by one unit. This rounding technique is applicable only when rounding real values to the nearest integer value. (There are also times when it is desired to change an integer value to a real value; an example is the statement Y=I. Here there is no problem of truncation.)

Figure 2-5 provides examples of arithmetic assignment statements. Note that a number of examples show an arithmetic expression in one mode whose results are to be assigned to a variable of the opposite mode. This is permissible, as explained previously, and is not to be considered in the same

Arithmetic Assignment Statements

An instruction to the computer to evaluate an expression and assign its numerical value to a variable name

General Form: VAR = EXPRESSION

Examples: PI = 3.1416

                          CIR = PI*R

                          AREA = PI*R**2

                          N = N+1

Arithmetic Assignment Statement	Value Assigned to Variable
J = 3*4+1	J is 13
C = 3*4+1	C is 13.
I = 4.∅/3.∅	I is 1
A = 4/3	A is 1.
X = 5.∅*3.∅/2.∅	X is 7.5
L = 5.∅*3.∅/2.∅	L is 7
M = 5*3/2	M is 7
B = 5*3/2	B is 7.
K = (5.∅*3.∅/2.∅)+∅.5	K is 8
N = (3.∅/4.∅)+∅.5	N is 1
J = (5.∅/4.∅)+∅.5	J is 1

FIG. 2-5
Arithmetic assignment statements.

category as a mixed-mode expression. The discussion of mixed modes given in Sec. 2-3c applies to the arithmetic expression portion of an arithmetic assignment statement.

2-8
TYPE-DECLARATION STATEMENTS

The computer identifies integer and real variables by the first letter in their names. However, for various reasons, the programmer may wish to use a variable name that does not start with the appropriate letter designator or may desire to change the mode of a variable named in a program written previously. The mode of a variable can be defined, regardless of the first-letter designator, by using *type-declaration statements.* The general forms of type-declaration statements are

INTEGER list of variables

REAL list of variables

In the case of the INTEGER statement, the value of each variable named in the list is treated as an integer value regardless of the first letter in the variable's name. The variables named in the list must be separated by commas. In the case of the REAL statement, the value of each variable named in the list is treated as a real value regardless of the first letter in the variable's name.

Examples of these statements are

INTEGER A, DELTA, LAST

REAL B, LOAD, MASS

The two statements tell the computer that the variables A and DELTA are to be integer values. Similarly the variables LOAD and MASS are to be real values. The variable LAST could have been omitted from the INTEGER statement and the variable B could have been omitted from the REAL statement because the letter designators already identify their type. However, it is not wrong to list them, and some programmers like to declare the mode of all variables in a program. The type-declaration statement is a nonexecutable statement and must appear in the program before any executable statement. Executable and nonexecutable statements are discussed in Sec. 2-9.

2-9
EXECUTABLE AND NONEXECUTABLE STATEMENTS

There are two general types of FORTRAN statements: *executable* and *nonexecutable* statements. The arithmetic assignment statement, discussed in Sec. 2-7, is an example of an executable statement. It instructs the computer to perform (execute) some specific action. Other types of executable statements are control statements, transfer statements, and input/output statements. These will be discussed in the following chapters.

Nonexecutable statements provide information to the computer that is essential for the proper execution of some executable statement. The type-declaration statement, discussed in Sec. 2-8, is an example of a nonexecutable statement. Declaring the variable DELTA to be an integer variable causes no action on the part of the computer, but it is essential to the proper execution of an assignment statement (or any other executable statement) which includes the variable name DELTA. Other types of nonexecutable statements are specification statements, definition statements, function statements, and FORMAT statements. With the exception of the FORMAT statements, all nonexecutable statements must appear in the program before any executable statement. Various nonexecutable statements will also be discussed in the following chapters.

2-10
STARTING THE PROGRAM

The procedures for running computer programs vary widely in different computer centers. All centers require one or more cards as the first card(s) in any program and sometimes other cards at the front of the group of data cards and at the end of the deck. These cards are known as the *job-control-language* (JCL) cards. The purpose of the JCL cards is to inform the computer of the name of the program, account number used for funding the program, programmer's name, and computer language required for the program.

Because these JCL requirements are unique to each computer center, no further mention of them will be made in the programs to be discussed. However, students must remember that JCL cards are a necessary part of each program and determine what the requirements are for particular computer centers.

2-11
ENDING THE PROGRAM

A rudimentary knowledge of arithmetic expressions and arithmetic assignment statements is sufficient for the student to begin writing simple programs. However, one more topic should be discussed first: After all instructions have been completed, FORTRAN requires the programmer to inform the computer that the program is complete. This operation is done by the statements STOP or CALL EXIT. Which statement to use depends on the procedure at the computer center which is determined locally. In any event, either STOP or CALL EXIT must be the next-to-last statement. The last statement must be END, which informs the computer that all the program has been read and to prepare the program for execution.

2-12
A TYPICAL FORTRAN PROGRAM

A FORTRAN program[1] to compute the circumference and area of a circle may now be written:

JCL CARD(S)	As appropriate to local procedure
PI=3.14159	Value 3.14159 assigned to variable name PI
RADIUS=10.0	Value 10.0 assigned to variable RADIUS
CIRCUM=PI*RADIUS*2.	Computes circumference and assigns value to variable name CIRCUM
AREA=PI*RADIUS**2	Computes area and assigns value to variable name AREA
STOP	Informs computer that calculations are complete
END	Informs the computer that all the program has been read and to prepare for execution

The AREA calculation shows one valid use of an apparent mixed-mode expression. The variables PI and RADIUS are real, while the constant 2 is an

---

[1] This program contains faults and should not be copied. These faults are discussed in Sec. 3-1.

integer. This is permissible in FORTRAN and, in this case, preferred. Using the integer value will tell the computer that the exponentiation of RADIUS can be done by multiplying it by itself. If the real constant (2.) were used, it would cause the computer to use a more time-consuming (hence, more costly) method of exponentiation. Fractional exponents must be real numbers, of course. However, integer numbers (or variables) must have integer exponents.

PROBLEMS

2-1
What are the results of the following integer operations?

a $8 \div 2$
b $6 \div 10$
c $(6 + 8) \div 5$

d $4 \times 5 \div 3 \div 2$
e $(4 \times 5) \div (3 \div 2)$
f $(4 \times (5 \div 3)) \div 2$

2-2
Express the following numbers in FORTRAN exponential form.

a 10.3
b 2345.7
c 378.66

d 0.453
e 0.00056
f 0.00678

2-3
Which of the following variable names are acceptable integer variables? If not, why not?

a JACK
b NEG5X
c PREFER

d I*JACK
e OPTION2
f INTEGRAL

2-4
Which of the following variable names are acceptable real variables?

a ACTION
b BETA/2
c OPTION2

d LITTLE
e XRAY
f HEIGHT

2-5
Write the following algebraic expressions as FORTRAN expressions.

a $\dfrac{a^2 + b^2}{c}$

e $\dfrac{a^2 y^b}{c} + e$

b $a^2 b - \dfrac{b^2 c}{d}$

f $(ab + ac) \div d^4$

c $3(x^2 y - y^2)$

g $a \div b + \dfrac{b - c}{d} \quad \dfrac{e^5}{f}$

d $4x^{a+b}$

h $(x^2 + y^2)^3 - 5ab + 2a \div 3b$

2-6

Write the following algebraic equations as FORTRAN arithmetic assignment statements.

a $R = \dfrac{Pb^3}{l^2}(3a + b)$

c $S = vt + \dfrac{at^2}{2}$

b $X = 2\pi fY - \dfrac{1}{2}fc$

d $F = \dfrac{Wv^2}{gr}$

2-7

Write the FORTRAN program necessary to compute the lateral surface area and volume of a rectangular box whose width is X, length is Y, and height is Z.

2-8

Write the FORTRAN program necessary to compute the surface area and volume of a sphere whose diameter is D.

2-9

Write the FORTRAN program necessary to compute the initial velocity and present displacement of a body moving in uniformly accelerated motion whose velocity at time T is V and whose acceleration is A.

GETTING 3.
INFORMATION
IN AND OUT

3-1
INTRODUCTION

The program for computing the circumference and area of the circle presented in Chap. 2, Sec. 2-12, has two major faults: First, the program as written is a waste of computer time since the calculations are performed only once. It takes time to prepare a program, and the computer time necessary to run a program is quite expensive. One would do better to solve the problem by hand. It is not economical to use a computer for such a problem unless the circumference and area for many radii are to be determined. Doing the same calculations repeatedly is called *iteration.* Revising the program of Chap. 2 as an iterative operation will be the topic of Chap. 4. Use of the computer is also indicated when the computations are so complex and so long that an unreasonable amount of time would be required to perform the operations by hand.

The second major fault in the program presented in Chap. 2 is that there is no provision for getting the results out of the computer in a usable form. The purpose of this chapter is to describe how information can be put into the computer and how results can be printed out, which requires more FORTRAN statements. It is critically important that these and all other statements be written exactly as described and illustrated in the examples; one extra comma, one unbalanced parentheses, one less period, or a misspelled FORTRAN word will cause a reading error and rejection of the program by the computer.

As stated in Chap. 1, there are several ways by which information can be put into and printed out of the computer. Since the input and output units usually available to the beginning student are the card reader and printer, the discussion in this text will be confined to these two units.

3-2
READ STATEMENTS

The READ statement is used to instruct the computer to cause the card reader to read a data card and place in storage the indicated value(s). The general form for the READ statement is

READ(*i,n*)A,X,J

In this statement, *i* is an integer number designating the input device—the card reader in our case; *n* is an integer number identifying another statement (the FORMAT statement) which specifies how the values are to be read and stored; and A,X,J represent variable names (referred to as a *list*) to which individual values so read are to be assigned.

The integer to use for *i* varies with different computer centers. The programmer must ascertain what is used in the local computer center. The digit 1 will be used to designate the card reader in the programs used in this text, but it is very important to remember that this may not be true at every computer installation; for example, the digit 5 is also commonly used to designate the card reader.

The integer number *n* is the choice of the programmer. This is a statement number identifying the FORMAT statement associated with the READ statement. What is a statement number? In many situations, one statement within a program must refer to another statement within the program. To do so, the statement to which reference is made must be identified by a statement number. Exactly how this is done and where it is punched on the statement card will be described later in this chapter.

The variable list is also the choice of the programmer. Each variable name in the list must conform to the mode (integer or real) of the value to be read: integer names for integer values and real names for real values. The number of variable names in the list should be the same as the number of values punched in the data card, although allowable variations of this generalization will be discussed later.

An example of a READ statement is

READ(1,100)RADIUS

Which means that one real value is to be read from a data card in the card reader and its value assigned to the variable name RADIUS. The data card is read according to instructions contained in statement 100. Another example is

READ(1,150)ALPHA,BETA,LAST

Here three values are to be read from one data card in the card reader. The first two values are real values and will be assigned, respectively, to the variable names ALPHA and BETA. The third value is an integer value and will be assigned to the variable name LAST. Statement 150 will specify how the data card is to be read. Figure 3-1 illustrates the elements of the READ statement.

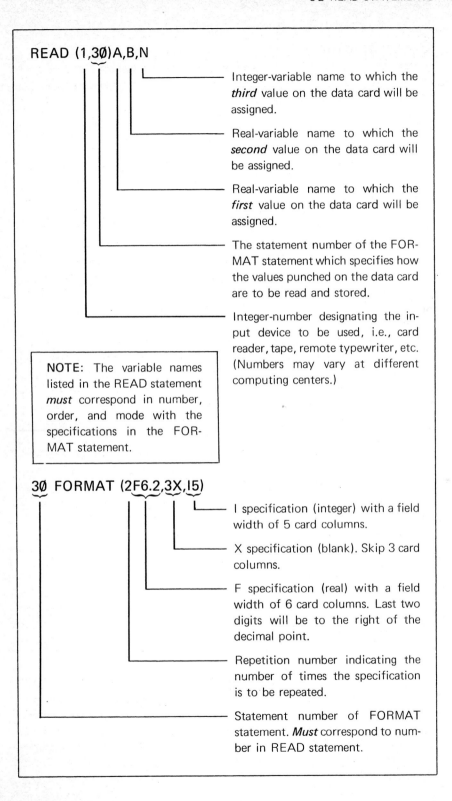

READ (1,3Ø)A,B,N

Integer-variable name to which the *third* value on the data card will be assigned.

Real-variable name to which the *second* value on the data card will be assigned.

Real-variable name to which the *first* value on the data card will be assigned.

The statement number of the FORMAT statement which specifies how the values punched on the data card are to be read and stored.

Integer-number designating the input device to be used, i.e., card reader, tape, remote typewriter, etc. (Numbers may vary at different computing centers.)

NOTE: The variable names listed in the READ statement *must* correspond in number, order, and mode with the specifications in the FORMAT statement.

3Ø FORMAT (2F6.2,3X,I5)

I specification (integer) with a field width of 5 card columns.

X specification (blank). Skip 3 card columns.

F specification (real) with a field width of 6 card columns. Last two digits will be to the right of the decimal point.

Repetition number indicating the number of times the specification is to be repeated.

Statement number of FORMAT statement. *Must* correspond to number in READ statement.

FIG. 3-1
READ statement.

3-3

FORMAT STATEMENTS

A FORMAT statement is the statement that specifies how the data card will be read. It also is used to specify how the results of calculations will be printed. If the READ statement is

READ(1,1ØØ)RADIUS

then the associated FORMAT statement could be

1ØØ FORMAT(F1Ø.3)

The 1ØØ is the statement number identifying the FORMAT statement referred to in the READ statement. The specification contained within the parentheses specifies how the value is to be read. Figure 3-1 also illustrates the elements of the FORMAT statement.

3-4

F SPECIFICATIONS

The F1Ø.3 is an F specification and means that the value on the data card is to be a real value without an exponent (F) and will be read from the first ten (1Ø) columns of the data card. The 1Ø is called the *field width* and determines the number of card columns covered. There are three decimal places (.3). The decimal point need not be punched on the data card. The FORMAT statement will automatically place the decimal point between the seventh and eighth digits. However, usually it is advisable for the beginner to punch the decimal point in the data cards since this practice will override the specification in the FORMAT statement if the specification and data do not match. A decimal point punched in a card occupies a card column and must be included in the field width, thus reducing by one the number of digits that can be punched in a given field width.

If the READ statement is

READ(1,15Ø)ALPHA,BETA,LAST

the FORMAT statement might be

15Ø FORMAT(F1Ø.3,F5.Ø,I4)

As described previously the first specification is a real value without an exponent punched in card columns 1 to 1Ø. Of prime importance is the compatibility between the specification in the FORMAT statement and the variable name in the READ statement list. Any disparity in mode between these elements will cause trouble.

The F5.Ø means that the value for the second variable (BETA) is punched in the next 5 columns of the data card (columns 11 to 15), that it is a real number without an exponent, and that no decimal places are shown. The second specification and the second variable must correspond in mode. Note that specifications in the FORMAT statement are separated by a comma.

The above discussion assumes that the field width defined by the specification in the FORMAT statement and the actual field width occupied by the value punched in the data card are the same. If the defined and actual field widths vary, the value stored as a result of the READ statement may bear absolutely no resemblance to the value that the programmer intended. Hence extreme care must be exercised to insure that the field widths defined by the specification and actually occupied on the data card are identical. This requirement holds true for all types of specifications.

3-5
I SPECIFICATIONS

The I4 is an I specification and means that the third variable (LAST) is to be an integer value (I). Its value is punched in the next 4 columns of the data card (columns 16 to 19). No decimal point may be used in an I specification, and an integer number must be punched in the data card. Integer values must be right-justified within their field width since columns without a punch are read as zeros. For example, if an integer value is specified as I4 and the numbers 123 are punched in the three leftmost columns, the value of the number in the I4 field will be read as 1230; however, if the number were punched in the three rightmost columns, the value 0123 would be read. The zero does not change the value in this situation. The third specification and the third variable mode must correspond. Figure 3-2 illustrates additional examples of READ and FORMAT statements.

3-6
REPEATING SPECIFICATIONS

If the field widths of the first two numbers on the data card were identical, the FORMAT statement would read

150 FORMAT(2F10.3,I4)

The 2 preceding the F is a repetition number meaning, in this case, that the following specification is to be repeated twice. In other words, the first two values on the data card are each 10 columns wide with 3 decimal places.

3-7
X SPECIFICATIONS

The X specification means that a column is to be skipped. Through the use of a repetition number, any number of columns can be skipped. If the READ and FORMAT statements are

READ(1,200)CASH,LCAR
200 FORMAT(5X,F10.2,2X,I5)

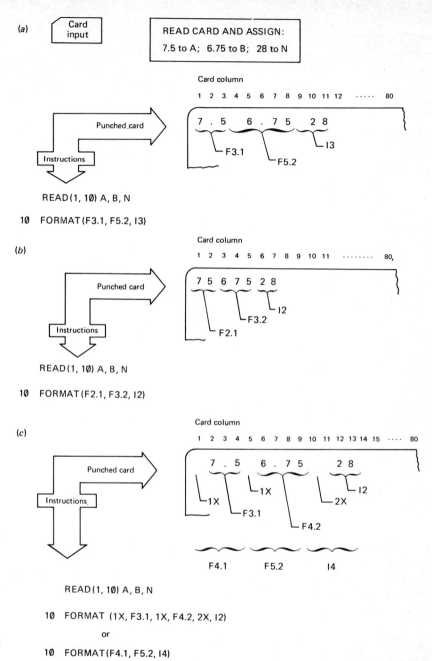

FIG. 3-2
Applications of READ and
FORMAT statements.

then the first 5 columns of the data card are skipped, a real value with 2 decimal places is read from the next 10 columns; then 2 more columns are skipped, and an integer value is read from the following 5 columns. Figure 3-2c illustrates additional examples.

3-8

WRITE STATEMENTS

The WRITE statement instructs the computer to print the desired results. The general form for the WRITE statement is

WRITE(i,n)A,X,J

In this statement, i is an integer number designating the output unit, n is an integer number identifying the statement number of the FORMAT statement that specifies how the results are to be printed, and A,X,J represents the list of variable names whose values are to be printed. As with the READ statement, the number identifying the printer varies from system to system. The digit 3 will be used throughout this text, although the digit 6 is also commonly used. Examples of the WRITE and FORMAT statements are

```
      WRITE(3,2ØØ)RADIUS,CIRCUM,AREA
2ØØ  FORMAT(1X,F1Ø.3,5X,F1Ø.3,5X,F1Ø.3)
```

The WRITE statement is similar to the READ statement. The important differences are in the associated FORMAT statement. The 1X in the FORMAT statement instructs the printer to skip the first print position on the printed sheet. The desirability of skipping the first print column will be discussed in Sec. 3-14. The first F1Ø.3 means that the first variable in the list (RADIUS) will be printed in the next 1Ø print positions with 3 decimal places. An important difference between input and output is that while the decimal point need not appear on the data card (though recommended), the decimal point always appears on the printout. Hence, the field width must include a print position (column) for the decimal point. As with the READ and its associated FORMAT, each specification and each variable to be printed must correspond in mode.

The 5X between the first and second F1Ø.3 means that the printer will skip 5 columns between the first and second variable values. The 5X between the second and the third F1Ø.3 serves the same purpose. Therefore, the programmer is sure that there will always be a fixed minimum number of spaces between the values on the same line of output. The same result could be achieved by increasing the field width to include the desired spaces: FORMAT (1X,3F15.3).

Although a number within the size limits of a particular computer can be read by the computer, printing that same number can cause problems. Figure 3-3 shows a simple program that specifies a number and then prints it with different specifications. The first WRITE and FORMAT statements resulted in the first line of data. Compare that value with the first line of the program which specified the value of X. The specified value is beyond the "word" limit of the computer, and hence a truncation has occurred, resulting in the value printed. The programmer must be aware of this possibility and needs to know the limitations of a particular computer.

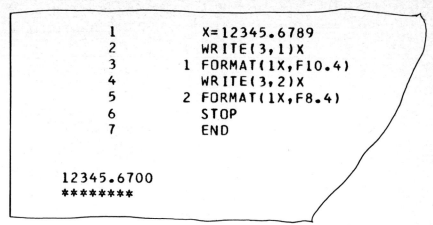

```
1          X=12345.6789
2          WRITE(3,1)X
3        1 FORMAT(1X,F10.4)
4          WRITE(3,2)X
5        2 FORMAT(1X,F8.4)
6          STOP
7          END


    12345.6700
    ********
```

FIG. 3-3
Printing with an F specification.

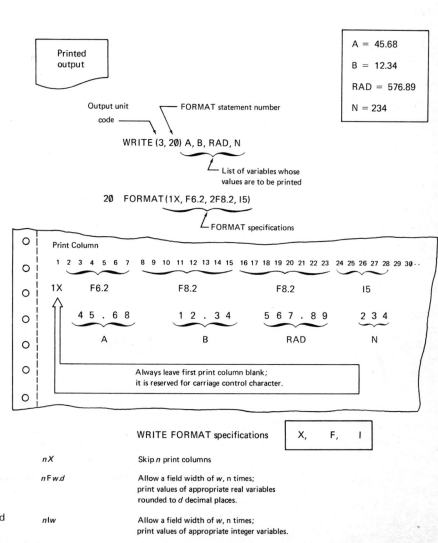

Printed output

A = 45.68

B = 12.34

RAD = 576.89

N = 234

Output unit code ———   ┌— FORMAT statement number

WRITE (3, 2Ø) A, B, RAD, N
                └—— List of variables whose
                      values are to be printed

2Ø   FORMAT(1X, F6.2, 2F8.2, I5)
                  └— FORMAT specifications

Print Column

1	2 3 4 5 6 7	8 9 10 11 12 13 14 15	16 17 18 19 20 21 22 23	24 25 26 27 28 29 30 --
1X	F6.2	F8.2	F8.2	I5
	4 5 . 6 8	1 2 . 3 4	5 6 7 . 8 9	2 3 4
	A	B	RAD	N

Always leave first print column blank;
it is reserved for carriage control character.

WRITE FORMAT specifications | X, | F, | I |

nX	Skip n print columns
nFw.d	Allow a field width of w, n times; print values of appropriate real variables rounded to d decimal places.
nIw	Allow a field width of w, n times; print values of appropriate integer variables.

FIG. 3-4
Applications of WRITE and FORMAT statements.

The second WRITE and FORMAT statements of Fig. 3-3 resulted in nothing but a row of stars (asterisks). This result is caused by an attempt to print a number larger than the one specified in the FORMAT and is a warning to use a larger field width in the specification. Some computer systems will print a value when the field width specification is too small, but with leading digits or characters dropped (truncated from left to right). Figure 3-4 illustrates an additional application of the WRITE and the FORMAT statements.

3-9

E SPECIFICATIONS

When the number of digits in a resulting value is uncertain or the value is likely to be very large or very small, it is often advantageous to use an E specification, for example

200 FORMAT(1X,3E16.7)

This specification causes the value to be printed as a real number with an exponent, in other words, as a decimal number between .1 and 1.∅ with a power of 1∅ exponent to show the actual magnitude of the value. A value printed by the specification E14.7 would appear as

b∅.1234567Eb∅3

where the b's represent blank spaces. If the number is negative, the first b is replaced by a minus sign, as shown in Fig. 3-5. If the number is less than 1, the second b is replaced by a minus sign, indicating a negative power of 1∅. It can be seen from the example that seven print positions are required in addition to the number of decimal positions specified. Therefore, the minimum field specification, if seven decimal positions are desired, would be E14.7. Since the specification in the FORMAT statement is E16.7, there will be two blanks between each of the three values to be printed.

Some programmers do not care to have results printed in this form but prefer values between 1.∅ and 1∅.∅. This can be accomplished by using a scale factor, which also increases the number of digits that can be printed in the same field width. Changing the specification to 1PE14.7 would cause that same value previously used to be printed as

b1.234567∅Eb∅2

Note that there are eight digits in the number and that the power of 1∅ has been reduced by one. The 1P is the scale factor. It tells the computer that the number as it exists within the computer should be multiplied by 1∅ and the exponent reduced accordingly. Other scale factors, such as 2P or 3P, can be used, but there is little advantage in so doing. When using the power factor, the preceding FORMAT statement is written

200 FORMAT(1X,1P3E16.7)

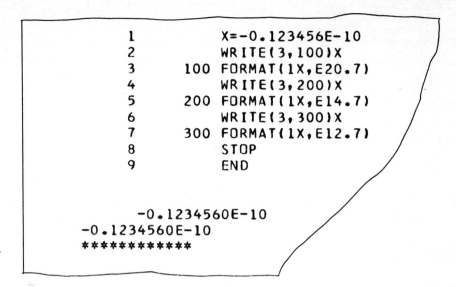

```
1              X=-0.123456E-10
2              WRITE(3,100)X
3      100 FORMAT(1X,E20.7)
4              WRITE(3,200)X
5      200 FORMAT(1X,E14.7)
6              WRITE(3,300)X
7      300 FORMAT(1X,E12.7)
8              STOP
9              END


         -0.1234560E-10
     -0.1234560E-10
     ************
```

FIG. 3-5
Printing with an E specification.

Note that scale factor is given first, then the number of such specifications, and then the actual specification. If a scale factor is used for an E specification and there are F specifications following, the scale factor will be applied to the F specifications also and strange results will occur. In this situation, a scale factor of ØP (zero P) should prefix the specification immediately following.

Figure 3-5 illustrates what happens in printing under the E specification. Line 1 of the program defines the value of X. The first WRITE and FORMAT statements resulted in the first value shown in the printout. Note the field width (2Ø) of the E specification allows 6 leading blank spaces. Compare the first line of output with the second line which begins in print column 2. The second WRITE and FORMAT statements, using an E specification of 14.7, resulted in the same value moved 6 print columns to the left. However, the third WRITE and FORMAT statements resulted in a row of 12 stars (the field width specified) because the field width was too small to accommodate the required number of digits. Not all computer systems will give this result. Some systems will truncate the value from left to right, dropping first the algebraic sign, then the leading zero, the decimal point, the next digit, etc., but printing the remaining digits to fill the specified field width. Such results can be grossly misleading.

The E specification is seldom used to input data unless the value to be read is too large (or too small) to be expressed in an F specification. The E specification is more commonly used in printing results, particularly when the magnitude of the value is uncertain.

3-10
A SPECIFICATIONS
The A specification permits the programmer to input, manipulate, and output

any characters (numeric, alphabetic, or special) recognized by the computer. These characters may be letters, digits, punctuation marks, and the character "blank;" therefore, they are often called *alphanumeric* characters. The A specification makes it possible to sort words alphabetically, compare words and/or numbers, and branch to specific statements depending on the comparison.

The exact number of characters n that can be stored in a "word," or storage location, depends upon the particular computer being used. It is important to know that number n in understanding what happens during input and output.

The general form of the A specification is Aw, where w is the number of characters to be stored in a given "word." On input, when w is equal to or greater than n, the rightmost n characters will be stored in the designated storage location. Hence, w should not exceed n except when special effects are desired and planned. When w is less than n, the w characters will be stored in the left portions of the storage location followed by sufficient blanks to complete the "word." The storage location is specified by a variable name.

For an example of inputting alphanumeric data, assume that a data card has *b*COMPUTER*b*GRAPHICS punched in the first 18 columns and that n is 4. The statements

        READ(1,1ØØ)A,B,C,D,E
    1ØØ FORMAT(4A4,A2)

will place *b*COM in storage location A, PUTE in location B, R*b*GR in location C, APHI in location D, and CS*bb* in location E.

On output, when w is greater than n, ($w - n$) blanks followed by the n characters in storage will be printed. Hence, as in input, w should not exceed n. When w is equal to or less than n, the leftmost w characters in storage will be printed. For an example of output, assume that the variables A, B, C, D, and E have the characters stored as read previously. The statements

        WRITE(3,2ØØ)A,B,C,D,E
    2ØØ FORMAT(1X,4A4,A2)

will print the following line:

*bb*COMPUTER*b*GRAPHICS

where the first *b* is caused by the 1X. If the FORMAT statement were

    2ØØ FORMAT(1X,5A4)

the printed result would be

*bb*COMPUTER*b*GRAPHICS*bb*

Consider the situation when the letters I, N, P, and S are punched in the first 4 columns of a data card and the card is read according to the following statements:

```
    READ(1,100)A,B,C,D
100 FORMAT(4A1)
```

The execution of the READ statement would result in I*bbb* in storage location A, N*bbb* in location B, P*bbb* in location C, and S*bbb* in location D. If printed by the statements

```
    WRITE(3,200)D,C,A,B
    WRITE(3,200)C,A,B
    WRITE(3,200)B,A,C,D
200 FORMAT(1X,4A1)
```

the words *b*SPIN, *b*PIN, and *b*NIPS will be printed on successive lines of the output sheet.

When using the A specification, the programmer first must know how many characters can be stored in a "word" and then must be very careful of the field widths specified. Excessive field widths should be used only when the results of that width are desired and planned.

Care must be exercised in the choice of variable names when using the A specification. It may make no difference which letter is the first letter of the variable's name with some computers and in some applications. However, if these alphanumeric characters are to be moved about from one variable to another, the two variable names must be compatible. These alphanumeric characters are identified in storage by binary digits (0s and 1s) just as any other number. There is a difference in internal storage arrangement between an integer "word" and a real "word" in the storage unit. Because of these two facts, some interesting and unexpected results can occur when an alphanumeric character or string of alphanumeric characters stored in the location BOB is moved to the storage location JOHN. The beginning programmer is well advised to use integer-variable names for alphanumeric characters.

3-11
UNFORMATTED READ STATEMENTS

The unformatted READ statement is not a standard part of FORTRAN IV, but it is available in those installations using the WATFIV compiler program. When available, it provides a simpler but less flexible method of inputting data than when using the FORMAT statements discussed in Sec. 3-3. The general form of the unformatted READ statement is

READ,A,X,J

A,X,J represents a list of variable names to which numerical values read from data cards are to be assigned. This list must be identical in number and mode with the values punched on the data card(s) to be read by this statement. The individual values on the cards are separated by commas, though in some versions they may be separated by blanks. Real values may be punched with or without an exponent. Note that only integer and real values may be read; alphanumeric input is not available. Also it is not possible to read selected data from a card and skip over other data on that card.

3-12
UNFORMATTED WRITE (PRINT) STATEMENTS

The unformatted WRITE statement is available in those installations which permit the unformatted READ statement. The general form of the WRITE statement is

PRINT,A,X,J

A,X,J represents a list of variable names whose values are to be printed. Variable names in this list must be in the same mode as the values to be printed. Some blank spaces will be automatically placed between successive values. If the list of variable names is long, the corresponding output may require more than one line, which is done automatically. The number of values that will be printed on one line varies with versions of FORTRAN that permit this statement. The user must ascertain what is provided at a particular computer center.

The specifications used by the PRINT statement are, for practical purposes, an E17.7 for real values and an I13 for integer values. This means that a field of real values will be separated from the preceding value by four blanks if the real value is positive and three blanks if the value is negative. Since the largest integer value can consist of about ten digits (Sec. 2-3a), a field of integer values will be separated from the preceding value by a minimum of two blanks if the integer value is negative and three blanks if the value is positive. Since integers are right-justified in their field, the number of blanks will increase as the number of digits in the integer value decreases. Knowing how various values will be printed by the PRINT statement is essential if column headings are desired.

3-13
COLUMN HEADINGS

Results printed without identification are often difficult to read without referring back to the WRITE statement to relate printed values with variable names. Printing column headings, units, or other identifying remarks along with the numerical values eliminates this problem. There are two methods for printing alphabetic information with the numerical values: the Hollerith and literal specifications:

a Hollerith Specification The general form for the Hollerith specification is

*w*H list of characters

where w is an integer number corresponding to the number (count) of characters, including blanks, in the list immediately following the letter H. These characters are printed in the print position specified by the Hollerith specification in the FORMAT statement. For example, consider the statements

```
    WRITE(3,100)
100 FORMAT(3X,13HCIRCUMFERENCE)
```

Note that there is no list of variable names in the WRITE statement; but since the associated FORMAT statement contains no specifications for variables, no such list is required. The FORMAT statement instructs the printer to skip the first three print columns (3X) and print the 13 characters following the H in print positions 4 to 16. Care must be exercised when using the Hollerith specification to make w equal to the number of characters (including blanks or spaces) to be printed. This means the programmer must count the characters carefully. An error in counting will cause the program to be rejected by the computer.

Another example of a WRITE statement employing the Hollerith specification is

```
    WRITE (3,200)X,Y
200 FORMAT(1X,7HWHEN X=,F6.2,8H THEN Y=,F6.2)
```

These statements will print the output in sentence form with numerical values inserted where the F specifications appear. Examination of the FORMAT statement will show that where blanks (spaces) occur in a Hollerith field they are counted as characters.

b Literal Specification The literal specification has an advantage over the Hollerith specification in that the characters to be printed need not be counted. Using a literal specification, the FORMAT statement

```
100 FORMAT(3X,13HCIRCUMFERENCE)
```

would be

```
100 FORMAT(3X,'CIRCUMFERENCE')
```

The apostrophe character, available on the card punch, is used before and after the characters to be printed. All characters between the apostrophes are printed literally as they appear in the FORMAT statement. Using the literal specification, FORMAT statement 200, given previously, would be

```
200 FORMAT(1X,'WHEN X=',F6.2', THEN X=',F6.2)
```

The greater simplicity of the literal specification is apparent. But do not underestimate the usefulness of the Hollerith specification. There are occasions, such as those described in Sec. 3-14, where the H specification is needed.

3-14
CARRIAGE CONTROL

When the specifications of each FORMAT statement are satisfied (the right parenthesis is encountered), the typing carriage of the printer returns to the starting position (print column 1) and the paper is advanced to the next line. Often it is desirable to skip a line between lines of print. One way this can be done is through the use of a slash mark (/) in the FORMAT statement. The slash mark (/) referred to is the same character as the FORTRAN division symbol. Consider the following statements:

```
    WRITE(3,1ØØ)A,B,C
1ØØ FORMAT(1X,3F2Ø.3,/)
```

When the WRITE statement is executed according to its associated FORMAT statement, the carriage will return to print column 1 and the paper will advance to the next line when the slash (/) is encountered; then when a parenthesis is reached, indicating the end of the FORMAT statement, the carriage will attempt to return to the starting point again and the paper will advance to the next line. Therefore, a line has been skipped. A double slash (//) will skip two lines; a triple slash (///) will skip three lines, etc. Use of slash marks in this way is comparable to double or triple spacing on a typewriter.

A slash (/) can be used anywhere in the FORMAT statement if it is desired to print part of the results on one line and a later part on the next line. For example, the statements

```
    WRITE(3,2ØØ)A,B,C
2ØØ FORMAT(1X,F3.Ø,/,1X,F3.Ø,/,1X,F3.Ø,/)
```

will cause the numerical values A, B, and C to be printed on three successive lines, each beginning in print column 2. The last slash mark preceding the right parenthesis will move the printer carriage back to print column 1, skip a line, and await further instructions. It should be noted that the FORMAT statement can also be written as

```
2ØØ FORMAT(3(1X,F3.Ø,/))
```

See Fig. 3-6a and b for examples of the use of the slash mark.

Sometimes data must be printed while the WRITE statement is under iterative control and where it is not desired to skip lines between data but it is desired to skip a line before printing out the next group of data. The Hollerith specification can be used for this type of carriage control. In every FORMAT statement used previously, the first print position has been skipped by including a 1X as the first specification. The first print column (position)

(a) If   A = 13.   B = 21.   C = 35.

then   WRITE(3,2Ø)A,B,C,
            2Ø FORMAT(1X,F3.Ø,/,1X,F3.Ø,/,1X,F3.Ø,/)

which will result in:

Print column

```
1 2 3 4 5 6 7 8 9 10 11 12 . . .
1 3 .
2 1 .
3 5 .
```

(b) If   A = 127.3452   B = 3.5278   I = 3241

then   WRITE(3,3Ø)A,B,I
            3Ø FORMAT(1ØX,F1Ø.4,/,1ØX,F1Ø.4,/,11X,I4)

which will result in:

Print column

```
1 2 3 4 5 6 7 8 9 10 11 12 13 14 15 16 17 18 19 20 21 22 . . .
                  1 2 7 . 3 4 5 2
                        3 . 5 2 7 8
            3 2 4 1
```

FIG. 3-6
Example of slash mark used for carriage control.

is reserved for carriage control. If a zero character appears in the print position, the paper is advanced to the next line and the zero character is not printed (suppressed). However, in the present case, it is desired to skip a line after a series of single-spaced data. The slash mark (/) described previously cannot be used in the FORMAT statement controlling the printing of the data because its presence would skip a line between each line of data, which is not desired. Consider the following statements:

```
    WRITE(3,2ØØ)
2ØØ FORMAT(1HØ)
```

These two statements deliberately try to print a zero in the first print position. The zero in the first print column will cause the paper to be advanced one line, and the right parenthesis will advance the paper another line. The result is that two lines are skipped (double spacing). The zero is not printed.

On some occasions, it might be desired to print different portions of the results on separate pages. If the digit 1 appears in the first print position, the paper is advanced to the top of the next page. The digit 1 is not printed. Consider the statements

FIG. 3-7
Keyboard for IBM 029 card
punch *(Courtesy of IBM).*

```
     WRITE(3,25Ø)
25Ø FORMAT(1H1)
```

The attempt to print the digit 1 in the first print position causes the printer to advance the paper to the top of the next page. The digit 1 is not printed. The importance of reserving the first print position by use of the X specification, or increased field width, to prevent the inadvertent attempt to print the digits Ø or 1 in the first print position, with unexpected results, should now be evident.

3-15
PREPARING INSTRUCTION AND DATA CARDS

All instruction and data cards are prepared (punched) using the card (or key) punch. (*Card punch* and *key punch* are different names for the same piece of equipment illustrated in Fig. 1-3.) This machine will punch holes in standard (3.25 X 7.375 in.) computer cards (sometimes called *Hollerith cards*). Knowledge of how these holes represent various characters and of the details of their interpretation by the computer is not necessary for the beginning programmer and therefore will not be discussed in this text. It is sufficient to accept the fact that the card punch will punch holes which can be identified as specific characters by the computer.

The heart of the card punch is the keyboard, shown in Fig. 3-7. Depressing the proper key will cause the machine to make the corresponding punches in

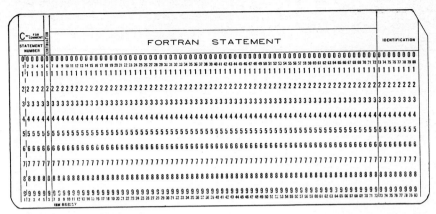

FIG. 3-8
Statement card.

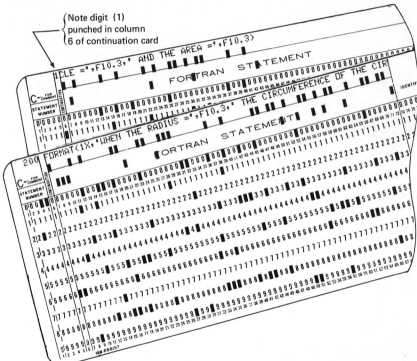

FIG. 3-9
Statement card with a
continuation.

the card. The operation of the card punch is best learned by experience. Brief
instructions on the basic operation of the card punch (the IBM 029 Printing
Card Punch) are included in Appendix B.

Most computer centers supply FORTRAN instruction and data cards,
marked differently. Actually the cards can be used interchangeably. It is only
the position of the punches that is important. However, it is helpful for the
beginner to use the card identified for the specific purpose.

A FORTRAN statement card is illustrated in Fig. 3-8. Note that the first 5
columns are reserved for the statement number, which may be punched
anywhere in the 5-column field. Some programmers prefer to start all numbers
in column 1; thus, the statement numbers are left-justified. Others prefer to

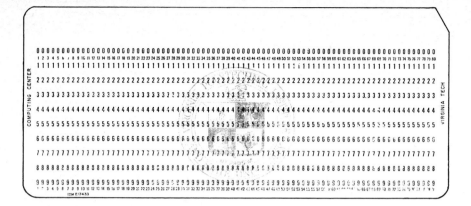

FIG. 3-10
Data card.

use the rightmost positions; thus, the statement numbers are right-justified. Either way is acceptable. The FORTRAN statement is punched in the card starting in column 7. No statement can extend beyond column 72. If the statement is not completed by column 72, the statement must be continued on the next card. This is done by punching a nonzero character, usually a 1, in column 6 of the next card and continuing the statement starting in column 7, as shown in Fig. 3-9. Columns 73 to 80 of the instruction card can be used in any way desired by the programmer other than as a part of the instruction. These columns are ignored by the computer, and normally they are not used by the programmer.

A data card is illustrated in Fig. 3-10. All 80 columns can be used for data. The only restriction is that the data must be punched to conform to the specifications in the FORMAT statement accompanying the appropriate READ statement. If the unformatted READ statement is used, each item of data must be separated by a comma or blank. With the exception of alphanumeric data to be used with the A specification, no alphabetic or special character should be punched in a data card. Digits and decimal points representing numerical values are the only characters which may be punched in a data card unless reading with the A specification. The only exceptions are the commas separating data items when used with the unformatted READ statement and the + or − signs. Data cards containing any other characters will be rejected by the computer.

3-16
COMMENT CARDS

When reviewing an old program or studying a program prepared by someone else, a problem frequently encountered is trying to recall or understand why some particular technique or procedure was used. Some explanatory comments are often included with the program listing to eliminate or reduce this problem. These comments are punched in comment cards which become part of the program deck. A comment card is simply an instruction or data card with the letter C punched in card column 1, as illustrated in Fig. 3-11. All 79 of the remaining columns can be used for a verbal explanation, or comment.

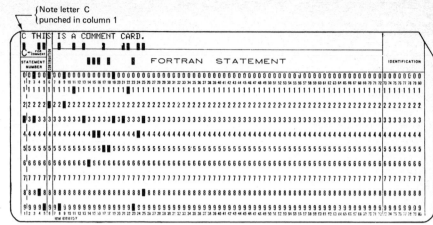

FIG. 3-11
Statement card used as a comment card.

```
      1           READ(1,100)RADIUS
      2      100  FORMAT(F10.3)
           C PUT IN VALUE OF PI.
      3           PI=3.14159
           C NOW CALCULATE THE CIRCUMFERENCE.
      4           CIRCUM=PI*RADIUS*2.0
           C NOW CALCULATE THE AREA.
      5           AREA=PI*RADIUS**2
           C NOW PRINT OUT RESULTS.
      6           WRITE(3,200)RADIUS,CIRCUM,AREA
      7      200  FORMAT(1X,'WHEN THE RADIUS =',F10.3,' THE CIRCUMFERENCE OF THE CIR
                 1CLE =',F10.3,' AND THE AREA =',F10.3)
      8           STOP
      9           END


WHEN THE RADIUS =    25.000 THE CIRCUMFERENCE OF THE CIRCLE =    157.079 AND THE AREA =   1963.494
```

FIG. 3-12
Circle problem.

Any character available on the card punch may be used. A comment card is printed exactly as punched and in sequence according to its position in the card deck, but it is ignored by the computer insofar as program instructions are concerned. If more than one comment card is used in sequence, a C must be punched in card column 1 of each card. The C is printed.

3-17
THE CIRCLE PROBLEM REVISITED

Now that it is known how to get information in and out of the computer, the program to calculate the circumference and area of a circle presented in Sec. 2-11 can be revised so as to read in data and print results. The revised program and results are shown in Fig. 3-12. Note the use of comment cards to explain each statement as the program progresses. Computer solution to this problem still cannot be justified since the program will calculate only values for a circle with a constant radius. How to further revise the program to calculate values for a circle with a variable radius will be discussed in Chap. 4.

3-18

PACKING STATEMENTS ON A CARD

Many program decks become quite thick and consequently are awkward to carry around. There are also times when several short statements occur in succession. In either case it is possible to "pack" the instruction card, or, in other words, put more than one statement on a card with each statement separated by a semicolon. The WATFIV compiler program contains a sub-routine called FIVPACK that will read a given program and punch cards with instructions packed. Packing may also be accomplished by hand during the initial preparation of the card deck.

Consider the following portion of a program:

```
A=B*X
WRITE(3,1ØØ)A
B=B+1.Ø
X=X+2.Ø
```

All the statements on these four cards can be packed on one card by using semicolons:

```
A=B*X;WRITE(3,1ØØ)A;B=B+1.Ø;X=X+2.Ø
```

The advantage of this procedure is obvious: It saves cards and reading time. By using continuation cards, a long program can be condensed on just a few cards. The disadvantage is that the printout of the program will appear exactly as the cards are set up, which makes reading the program more difficult. If programming errors occur, it is not immediately obvious which statement caused the error. When the error is found, the entire card must be repunched instead of correcting one statement on a single card and substituting that card in the deck.

When a long program involving statement numbers and FORMAT statements is to be packed, there are other rules to remember: Statements are separated by semicolons, as stated previously. Statement numbers are followed by a colon. FORMAT statements should be moved to the end of the program and cannot be packed. All comment cards should be removed as they also cannot be packed. Packing is done on the card in columns 7 to 72. If the statements to be packed require more than one card, they can be continued on the next card provided a character is punched in column 6 to signify a continuation. Since packing is done to conserve space, blanks are removed from all statements except where they are embedded with apostrophes. If a statement is completed near column 72, the semicolon is omitted and the packing is continued on the next card without a continuation mark in column 6.

Figure 3-13 illustrates how the program of Fig. 3-12 would be written in packed form. Notice that the comment cards have been removed and that the FORMAT statements are not packed. Of special interest is the line numbering of the computer-prepared program listing. In the normally prepared program,

```
    1          READ(1,100)RADIUS;PI=3.14159;CIRCUM=PI*RADIUS*2.0;AREA=PI*RADIUS**
              12;WRITE(3,200)RADIUS,CIRCUM,AREA
    6      100 FORMAT(F10.3)
    7      200 FORMAT(1X,'WHEN THE RADIUS =',F10.3,' THE CIRCUMFERENCE OF THE CIR
              1CLE =',F10.3,' AND THE AREA =',F10.3)
    8          STOP;END


WHEN THE RADIUS =    25.000 THE CIRCUMFERENCE OF THE CIRCLE =    157.079 AND THE AREA =   1963.494
```

FIG. 3-13
Circle problem in a packed
form.

each statement is numbered consecutively, as in Fig. 3-12. However, in Fig. 3-13, the first card is numbered 1 and the next number that appears is 6. Apparently, this is a mistake. However, when the first packed card and its continuation are examined, it will be found that they contain five statements. The computer is programmed to count each instruction and remember it even though no line number is shown in the left margin. Thus, if an error is made in punching the AREA statement or in its execution, the error message would refer to line 4 as the statement where the error occurred.

For these reasons, packing is recommended only with programs that have been tested and will be used many times thereafter. For more details on packing, consult the local computer center.

3-19
THE DATA STATEMENT
The DATA statement is a nonexecutable statement which allows the programmer to assign values to a list of variables. The general form of the DATA statement is

DATA A,B,C,I,J/a,b,c,k*n/

where A, B, C, I, and J represent a list of variable names to which values are to be assigned and a, b, c, and n represent the corresponding values. When $k*n$ is used, it means that the next k variables in the list (I and J) are to be assigned the same value: n. Note that in this case * does not indicate multiplication but that the value following is to be used k times. The value for k is always an integer number.

An example of the DATA statement is

DATA A,B,C,M,N/2.4,4.5,1.45,2*4/

Here the value 2.4 is given to the variable A; 4.5 to the variable B; 1.45 to the variable C; and 4 to both variables M and N. The variable names must correspond in number, mode, and relative position with the numerical values. As with other nonexecutable statements, the DATA statement must appear in the program prior to the first executable statement.

The main reason for introducing the DATA statement at this point in the discussion of FORTRAN is to allow the student to use the example programs given in this text on local systems without extensive changes. As indicated previously, some computer centers identify the card reader by the integer 1 and the printer by the integer 3. However, at other installations, different number codes may be used. Therefore, in all succeeding programs used as examples, the input or output device referred to in the READ or WRITE statements will be identified by a variable whose value is first assigned by a DATA statement. Thus, any program in this text can be converted to the reader's system by changing only one statement, the DATA statement. For example, the statements

```
DATA ICR,IPR/1,3/
READ(ICR,100)A,B,C
WRITE(IPR,200)A,B,C
```

give the same results as

```
READ(1,100)A,B,C
WRITE(3,100)A,B,C
```

The variable names ICR and IPR represent, respectively, an Integer number identifying the Card Reader and an Integer number identifying the PRinter. In this example, the integer identification numbers 1 and 3 were used; any other identification numbers, such as 5 and 6, can be used as required.

PROBLEMS
3-1
A data card is punched as follows:

124.56843.72*b*54.38*bb*7.85932

What values will be assigned to each of the given variables as the result of the following statements?

a READ(1,3)A,B,
   3 FORMAT(2F6.2)

b READ(1,4)A,B,C
   4 FORMAT(3F6.2)

c READ(1,5)A,B,C
   5 FORMAT(2F5.2,6X,F6.2)

d READ(1,6)A,B,C,D,LCAR
   6 FORMAT(4F7.3,I1)

e READ(1,7)A,B,I
   7 FORMAT(12X,2F6.2,1X,I2)

3-2
The following values are stored in the computer: $X=0.1234567E3$, $Y=0.4682E0$, $A=0.876543E-1$, $I=158$, $J=303$, and $K=5$. What will be printed as the result of the following statements?

a WRITE(3,1)X,Y
   1 FORMAT(2F10.3)

b WRITE(3,2)X,J
   2 FORMAT(1X,F8.4,I3)

c WRITE(3,3),X,Y,A,K
   3 FORMAT(1X,3F10.5,I6)

d WRITE(3,4)X
   4 FORMAT(F8.4)

e WRITE(3,5)X,A,I
   5 FORMAT(1X,F10.5,/,F10.5,I4)

3-3

Write a program to convert temperature expressed in degrees Celsius (°C) to degrees Fahrenheit (°F) and degrees Rankine (°R). The given temperature is 62.435°C and is punched on a data card occupying a field of 8 columns. Print the results as you desire.

3-4

Write a program to compute the area of the ring between two concentric circles whose radii are 159.34 and 79.40. Values for both radii are on the same card punched as consecutive digits without decimal points in columns 1 to 9. Print the results as you desire.

3-5

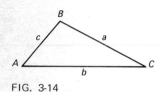

FIG. 3-14
Problem 3-5.

Figure 3-14 shows a triangle *ABC*. The cosine of an angle can be computed using the following formula: $\cos A = b^2 + c^2 - a^2/2bc$. The value of side *a* is 24.62, side *b* is 16.39, and side *c* is 33.00. Compute the value of the cosine for each of three angles (*A, B,* and *C*), and print on separate lines, skipping a line between each value. *Note:* The cosine of angle *C* should be negative. What does this signify?

TELLING 4.
THE COMPUTER
HOW TO DECIDE
AND REPEAT

4-1
INTRODUCTION

Chapters 2 and 3 have explained how to prepare arithmetic assignment statements that perform arithmetic operations and assign results to variable names and how to read data and print answers. To utilize the full power of the computer, it is necessary to know how to make the computer iterate and make basic decisions.

Iteration, or repetition of calculations, is termed *looping* and is accomplished through various transfer and control statements. A transfer statement is one that instructs the computer to transfer, or branch, to another statement designated by a unique statement number. A transfer statement may be either unconditional or conditional. An unconditional transfer statement always branches to a single designated statement while a conditional transfer statement may branch to one of several different designated statements, depending upon conditions of the data. Typical transfer statements are the GO TO and IF statements, which will be discussed in this chapter.

A control statement is one that causes the computer to repeat a given set of statements a specified number of times. The DO statement, discussed in this chapter, is a control statement.

4-2
THE GO TO STATEMENT

The GO TO statement is an unconditional transfer statement which always transfers control to a specified statement. The general form is

GO TO *n*

where n is an integer number corresponding to the statement number of the executable statement to which control is to be transferred. Control is always transferred to statement number n. An example of a GO TO statement is

GO TO 1∅

Every time this statement is encountered, control is transferred to statement number 1∅.

4-3
THE ARITHMETIC IF STATEMENT

The arithmetic IF statement is a conditional transfer statement which instructs the computer to examine a given value and transfer (branch) to some other statement, depending on the value or algebraic sign of the value in question. The general form of the arithmetic IF statement is

$$IF(V)n_1,n_2,n_3$$

where V is the value of any arithmetic expression and n_1, n_2, and n_3 are integer numbers designating up to three different statement numbers. V can be either a single variable name or the result of an arithmetic expression contained within the parentheses; it can be either an integer value or a real value. If V is *negative*, control is transferred to statement n_1; if V is *zero*, to statement n_2; and if V is *positive*, to statement n_3.

Branching when V is zero can lead to unexpected results. As discussed in Sec. 1-4, many real numbers cannot be stored as exact values. Hence, if the arithmetic expression represented by V involves real numbers, V may never be exactly zero. The programmer must always be aware of this possibility. No such problems occur if V is an integer value.

Examples of IF statements are

IF(A−B)5,1∅,15

If A is less than B, the value of the expression is negative and control is transferred to statement number 5; if A is equal to B, the value of the expression is apparently zero and control is transferred to statement number 1∅ (remember the problem which can occur if A is not exactly equal to B); and if A is greater than B, the value of the expression is positive and control is transferred to statement number 15.

IF(I−J)5,1∅,15

In this example the same transfers are made, but the transfers depend on integer values. There is no problem in this case when I is equal to J since the value of the expression is zero.

The three statement numbers need not be different. Consider a case where it is desired to transfer to statement number 5 when A is equal to or greater than zero and to statement number 1∅ when A is less than zero. For this condition, the IF statement is

IF(A)1∅,5,5,

A working example of the arithmetic IF statement is given in the program discussed in Sec. 4-7. Other examples can be found in the programs discussed in succeeding chapters. The best way to learn the use of the IF statement is to study how others have used it. (Another type of IF statement, known as the *logical IF,* will be discussed in Chap. 7.)

4-4
THE DO STATEMENT

The DO statement is a control statement which instructs the computer to repeatedly execute a portion of the program. The number of repetitions is defined by the specified minimum and maximum values of an automatically incremented integer variable. The general form of the DO statement is

DO *i* J=*k,l,m*

where *i* is an integer statement number which defines the range and J is an integer-variable name, known as the *index*, which varies from the lower limit value *k* to the upper limit value *l* in increments of *m*, where *k, l,* and *m* are integer constants or variables.

Consider these statements

```
  DO 3∅ I=1,7,2
  J=I**2
  WRITE(3,2∅)I,J
2∅ FORMAT(1X,2I5)
3∅ CONTINUE
```

The range of the DO statement includes all statements following the DO to and including statement number 3∅. The FORMAT statement may be within or outside of the range of the DO statement. The first time through the range I is set equal to 1. The value assigned to the index I is available for use as an integer variable within the loop. The value of I squared is assigned to the variable J, and then the values of both I and J (1 and 1) are printed. Having reached the end of the range, the computer will increment the value of the index variable I by 2, making it 3. The computer will then check to see if the index is greater than its upper limit (7); since I is less than 7, the range will be repeated again. The value of I^2 (9) is assigned to J, and the values of both I and J (3 and 9) are printed. The index will be incremented again by 2, making I = 5. Since I is still less than 7, the loop will be repeated. The value of I^2 (25) is assigned to J, and the values of I and J (5 and 25) are printed. The index is incremented again by 2, making it 7. Since 7 is equal to but not greater than the upper limit, the loop will be repeated again. When the index

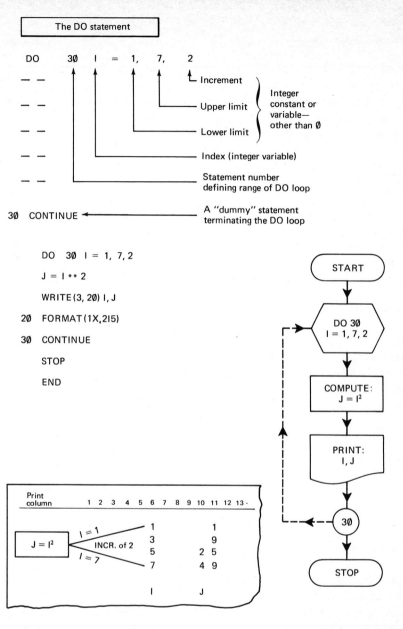

FIG. 4-1
DO statement.

is next incremented, it does become greater than the upper limit (7) and therefore control will be transferred automatically to the executable statement immediately following the last statement in the range. The results of this program are illustrated in Fig. 4-1.

When the index finally becomes greater than its upper limit, the DO statement is considered as satisfied and the value assigned to the index variable I is lost and no longer available for use. Because the number of times the range, or loop, is to be repeated depends solely upon the value of the index, there is a cardinal rule to remember: The value of the index *cannot* be changed within the range of the DO statement. It is essential that the programmer know how many times the loop will be repeated. A common error in the use of the DO statement is to repeat the loop one too few or one too many times.

The DO loop is used frequently with the value of the index incremented by 1. In this case, it is not necessary to provide a value for the increment since the absence of an incrementing value indicates to the computer that the increment is 1. An example is

DO 2∅ J=1,1∅

Here the loop through statement number 2∅ will be repeated for J = 1, 2, 3, 4, 5, 6, 7, 8, 9, 1∅. After the execution, when J = 1∅, J becomes 11, which is larger than its maximum value (1∅); therefore, control is transferred to the statement immediately following statement number 2∅.

Sometimes the programmer may wish to execute a DO loop a given number of times unless during some repetition a certain variable becomes too large (or too small) for a given condition. The following is an example of such a loop

```
   DO 4 K=1,15
   VAL=VAL**K
   IF(VAL−1∅∅∅.)4,4,6
4  ABLE=X+VAL
_ _ _ _ _ _ _ _ _ _ _ _ _ _
6  CAN=K
```

Here the DO loop through statement number 4 is to be executed 15 times. However, since the variable VAL comes from a preceding part of the program, it is uncertain what the value of VAL will be after exponentiation. In this example, the value of VAL should not exceed 1∅∅∅.∅. Therefore, the DO loop, as written, will be iterated normally unless the result of the expression in the IF statement is found to be positive. This occurs when the value of VAL is greater than 1∅∅∅.; control will be transferred to statement number 6, which is outside the range of the DO loop, and the execution of the loop will cease. In such a situation, an interesting side effect occurs: When control is transferred beyond the range of a DO loop before the DO loop is satisfied, the last value assigned to the index variable is retained and is available for subsequent use. Thus, in our current example, statement number 6, which is outside the range of the DO loop, will change the last integer value of the index K in the DO loop to the corresponding real value and assign that value to the variable name CAN.

4-5
THE CONTINUE STATEMENT
An important rule governing the use of the DO statement is that the terminating statement in the range of a DO must be an executable statement;

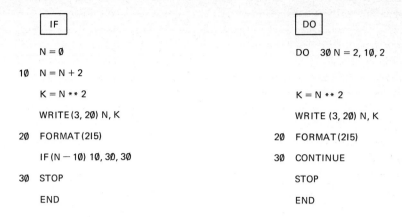

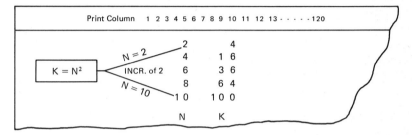

FIG. 4-2
Comparison of IF and DO loops.

however it cannot be a GO TO, an IF, or another DO statement. Neither can it be a STOP, CALL EXIT, or RETURN statement. (The RETURN statement will be discussed in Chap. 10.) However, the programmer may need to use one of the preceding statements as the final statement in the loop. This can be accomplished by adding a CONTINUE statement to the range of the DO. This statement, written simply as CONTINUE, is a dummy executable statement that results in no action by the computer; but it does satisfy the rule and still allows the last executable statement to be one that would not be permitted as a terminating statement.

There may be times when the loop is to be executed unless a given condition occurs before the DO statement is satisfied; when that condition occurs, the remaining statements in the loop are skipped and the loop is continued for other values. The CONTINUE statement enables the programmer to satisfy the preceding requirements. Consider the following simple example:

```
 8  DO 1Ø I=1,M
    IF(L−I)9,9,1Ø
 9  X=I
    SUM=SUM+X
1Ø  CONTINUE
```

The values of M, L, SUM, and Y come from READ or arithmetic assignment statements preceding the DO statement. The lower limit, upper limit, and increment of the index of a DO loop can be integer variables as long as their values have been defined or calculated earlier in the program. In this example, the upper limit of the index I is the value of the integer variable M.

As long as the value of the index I is greater than or equal to the value of the variable L, the subsequent statements are executed. If the value of the index is less than the value of L, control is transferred to the CONTINUE statement, which bypasses the intervening statements and allows the execution of the loop to continue. Note that if the IF statement had attempted to bypass the next two statements by transferring to the DO statement, the effect would have been to start the DO loop all over again with I = 1. Quite possibly this action could cause an endless loop, which obviously is undesirable. Figure 4-1 graphically shows the program presented first in Sec. 4-4 using the CONTINUE statement. Figure 4-2 shows how identical results can be obtained by looping under the control of either a DO statement or an IF statement.

4-6
NESTED DO LOOPS

It is possible to have DO loops within DO loops. This condition is called *nesting.* The new concepts introduced in using nested DO loops are included in the rules governing the use of DO loops:

1 The first statement in the range of a DO loop (the statement immediately following the DO statement) must be executable, which means that a specification statement, such as a FORMAT statement, cannot immediately follow the DO statement.

2 The last statement within the range of a DO loop (the terminating statement) must be an executable statement, but it must not be another DO statement or a GO TO, IF, STOP, CALL EXIT, RETURN, or END statement. The beginning programmer will often find that CONTINUE is the most suitable terminating statement.

3 In nesting DO loops it is permissible for the range of one DO loop (outer loop) to include the range of another DO loop (inner loop). This rule does not prevent nested DO loops from terminating with the same statement. Permissible nesting is shown schematically in Fig. 4-3.

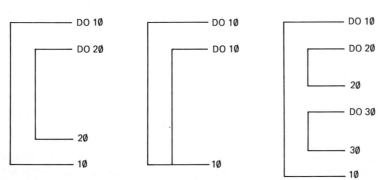

FIG. 4-3
Permissible nesting of DO loops.

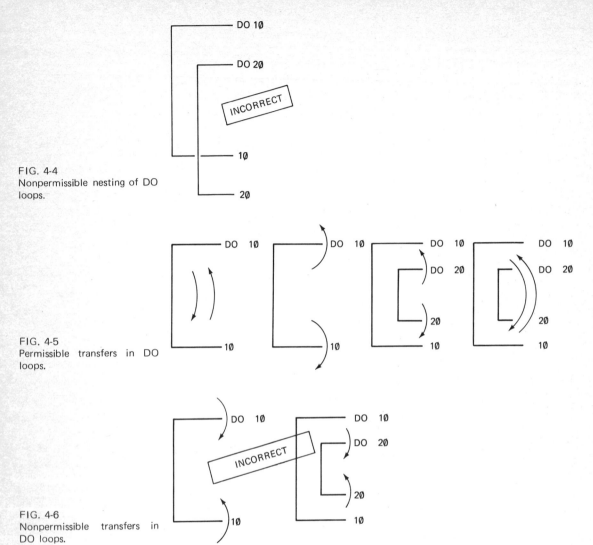

FIG. 4-4
Nonpermissible nesting of DO loops.

FIG. 4-5
Permissible transfers in DO loops.

FIG. 4-6
Nonpermissible transfers in DO loops.

4 It is not permissible for the range of an inner DO loop to extend beyond the range of an outer DO loop. This rule is illustrated in Fig. 4-4.

5 It is permissible to transfer from inside a DO loop to a statement outside the DO loop. This also means that with nested loops it is permissible to transfer from an inner DO loop to a statement in the outer DO loop. It is always permissible to transfer to a statement within the range of a given loop. This rule is illustrated in Fig. 4-5.

6 It is not permissible to transfer from outside the DO loop to a statement within the loop. This rule is shown schematically in Fig. 4-6.

7 It is not permissible for any statement within the range of a DO loop to change in any way the value of the index, its limits, or its increment. It is permissible to use the value of the index as it currently exists. See Fig. 4-7.

```
DO 10 I = M, K, L

I=A

READ, I

I=15

M=2

K=10

L=4
```

Statements of this type must not be used within the DO *loop.*

FIG. 4-7
Nonpermissible statements
within DO loops.

```
      1           DATA ICR,IPR/1,3/
      2           DO 1 I=1,46,5
      3           RADIUS=I
      4           PI=3.14159
      5           CIRCUM=PI*RADIUS*2.0
      6           AREA=PI*RADIUS**2
      7         1 WRITE(IPR,200)RADIUS,CIRCUM,AREA
      8       200 FORMAT(1X,'WHEN THE RADIUS =',F10.3,' THE CIRCUMFERENCE OF THE CIR
                 1CLE =',F10.3,' AND THE AREA =',F10.3)
      9           STOP
     10           END


 WHEN THE RADIUS =     1.000 THE CIRCUMFERENCE OF THE CIRCLE =      6.283 AND THE AREA =       3.142
 WHEN THE RADIUS =     6.000 THE CIRCUMFERENCE OF THE CIRCLE =     37.699 AND THE AREA =     113.097
 WHEN THE RADIUS =    11.000 THE CIRCUMFERENCE OF THE CIRCLE =     69.115 AND THE AREA =     380.132
 WHEN THE RADIUS =    16.000 THE CIRCUMFERENCE OF THE CIRCLE =    100.531 AND THE AREA =     804.247
 WHEN THE RADIUS =    21.000 THE CIRCUMFERENCE OF THE CIRCLE =    131.947 AND THE AREA =    1385.441
 WHEN THE RADIUS =    26.000 THE CIRCUMFERENCE OF THE CIRCLE =    163.363 AND THE AREA =    2123.715
 WHEN THE RADIUS =    31.000 THE CIRCUMFERENCE OF THE CIRCLE =    194.779 AND THE AREA =    3019.068
 WHEN THE RADIUS =    36.000 THE CIRCUMFERENCE OF THE CIRCLE =    226.194 AND THE AREA =    4071.501
 WHEN THE RADIUS =    41.000 THE CIRCUMFERENCE OF THE CIRCLE =    257.610 AND THE AREA =    5281.012
 WHEN THE RADIUS =    46.000 THE CIRCUMFERENCE OF THE CIRCLE =    289.026 AND THE AREA =    6647.602
```

FIG. 4-8
Circle problem with a DO loop.

8 Although rule 3 and Fig. 4-3 indicate that nested DO loops can terminate on the same statement, this rule is not always true. When more than two loops are so nested, particularly if there are statements between the various DOs, the computer is likely to become confused and reject the program. If this unhappy state occurs, simply use successive CONTINUE statements to terminate each loop.

4-7
THE CIRCLE PROBLEM AGAIN REVISITED

The statements presented in this chapter provide the flexibility to make the circle problem (discussed in Sec. 2-11 and revised in Sec. 3-17) into a much more realistic computer problem.

Assume that we want to calculate the circumference and area of 10 circles where the radius starts with a value of 1 and changes in increments of 5. A little thought establishes 46 as the upper limit. Since the index of the loop can be used for defining the values of the desired radii, there is no need to read these data from cards. Omitting the comment statements shown in Fig. 3-12 as no longer necessary, the program and its results are shown in Fig. 4-8.

```
 1              DATA ICR,IPR/1,3/
 2           1  READ(ICR,100)RADIUS,LCAR
 3         100  FORMAT(F10.3,I4)
 4              PI=3.14159
 5              CIRCUM=PI*RADIUS*2.0
 6              AREA=PI*RADIUS**2
 7              WRITE(IPR,200)RADIUS,CIRCUM,AREA
 8         200  FORMAT(1X,'WHEN THE RADIUS =',F10.3,' THE CIRCUMFERENCE OF THE CIR
               1CLE =',F10.3,' AND THE AREA =',F10.3)
 9              IF(LCAR)1,1,2
10           2  STOP
11              END
```

```
WHEN THE RADIUS =     1.000 THE CIRCUMFERENCE OF THE CIRCLE =     6.283 AND THE AREA =     3.142
WHEN THE RADIUS =     2.500 THE CIRCUMFERENCE OF THE CIRCLE =    15.708 AND THE AREA =    19.635
WHEN THE RADIUS =     4.750 THE CIRCUMFERENCE OF THE CIRCLE =    29.845 AND THE AREA =    70.882
WHEN THE RADIUS =     7.255 THE CIRCUMFERENCE OF THE CIRCLE =    45.584 AND THE AREA =   165.358
WHEN THE RADIUS =    10.333 THE CIRCUMFERENCE OF THE CIRCLE =    64.924 AND THE AREA =   335.430
WHEN THE RADIUS =    12.000 THE CIRCUMFERENCE OF THE CIRCLE =    75.398 AND THE AREA =   452.389
WHEN THE RADIUS =    15.000 THE CIRCUMFERENCE OF THE CIRCLE =    94.248 AND THE AREA =   706.858
WHEN THE RADIUS =    25.782 THE CIRCUMFERENCE OF THE CIRCLE =   161.993 AND THE AREA =  2088.250
WHEN THE RADIUS =    55.000 THE CIRCUMFERENCE OF THE CIRCLE =   345.575 AND THE AREA =  9503.309
WHEN THE RADIUS =   125.000 THE CIRCUMFERENCE OF THE CIRCLE =   785.397 AND THE AREA = 49087.340
```

FIG. 4-9
Circle problem with an IF
loop.

The disadvantage of this program is that while changing the parameters of the index will change the radii of circles that can be calculated, all increments of radii must be uniform. Also to change the number of circles to be calculated requires a new DO instruction.

A much more flexible program is shown in Fig. 4-9. The first thing to note in this program is the addition of a new variable (LCAR) to be read from the data card. Note the IF statement on line 9. When the value of LCAR is less than or equal to zero, the control is transferred to statement 1 and a new card is read. If a card is blank (has no punches) in a variable's field, that variable is assigned a value of zero. Hence, this program will continue to read cards simply by not punching anything in the field for the variable LCAR. When the last card desired to be read is prepared on the card punch, punching any positive integer value in the field for LCAR will cause the program to end after the calculations and printing are completed for the radius punched in the last card. This concept is often used when the number of data cards may vary with different computer runs.

4-8
OTHER CONTROL AND TRANSFER STATEMENTS
Many times it is desired to repeat the calculations of a program for as many sets of data as desired. If the number of repetitions is always the same, the program can be repeated under the control of a DO instruction. If the number of repetitions varies from time to time, the program can be repeated under the control of an IF statement, which tests to see if another data card is or is not present, as discussed in Sec. 4-7.

Another method of controlling the number of repetitions involves a variation of the READ statement. The form is

READ(i, n,END=m)A,X,J

```
  1            DATA ICR,IPR/1,3/
      C THIS IS A PROGRAM TO READ ANY ANGLE IN DEGREES, MINUTES, AND SECONDS
      C AND THEN TO CHANGE THE ANGLE TO A DECIMAL VALUE, AND THEN CONVERT
      C THE ANGLE TO RADIANS.
      C
      C PRINT COLUMN HEADINGS.
  2            WRITE(IPR,100)
  3      100 FORMAT(2X,'DEG MIN SEC     DECDEG       RADIANS',/)
      C
      C READ IN VALUES OF DEGREES, MINUTES, AND SECONDS AS DECIMAL NUMBERS.
      C TRANSFER TO STATEMENT 2 (STOP) WHEN ALL DATA IS READ.
  4        1 READ(ICR,200,END=2)A,B,C
  5      200 FORMAT(3F5.1)
      C
      C CONVERT THE ANGLE TO A DECIMAL VALUE.
  6            DECD=((A*3600.)+(B*60.)+C)/3600.
      C
      C CONVERT DECIMAL VALUE TO RADIANS.
  7            RAD=DECD*3.14159/180.
      C
      C CHANGE DECIMAL VALUES FOR DEGREES, MINUTES, AND SECONDS TO INTEGER
      C VALUES. TO SAVE SPACE, PACK INSTRUCTIONS ON ONE CARD.
  8            I=A;J=B;K=C
      C
      C PRINT INITAL ANGLE AND RESULTS OF CALCULATIONS.
 11            WRITE(IPR,300)I,J,K,DECD,RAD
 12      300 FORMAT(1X,3I4,F11.5,1PE14.5)
      C
      C CALCULATIONS COMPLETE, READ NEXT DATA CARD.
 13            GO TO 1
 14        2 STOP
 15            END


      DEG MIN SEC    DECDEG      RADIANS

      360   0   0   360.00000   6.28318E 00
      229  57  38   229.96050   4.01356E 00
      111   3   7   111.05190   1.93822E 00
       45   0   0    45.00000   7.85397E-01
       26  18  11    26.30305   4.59074E-01
        0   0   1     0.00028   4.84813E-06
```

FIG. 4-10
Degree-conversion program.

where i and n are (as before) integer values instructing the computer as to which input device to use and the statement number of the associated FORMAT statement; A,X,J represent the list of variable names.

The new item, END=m, will transfer control to statement number m when all data cards have been read. The use of this form of the READ statement is illustrated in Fig. 4-10. The choice of which method to use to loop through the READ statement depends on the programmer's preference and somewhat on the conditions of the particular program.

The statements previously discussed are not the only transfer or control statements available in FORTRAN IV. However, they are among the most commonly used statements and provide a sufficient flexibility of decision for the beginning programmer. Other transfer and control statements are given briefly in Table A-2.

4-9
SUMMARY

At this time it might be advisable to pause and review, through the means of an illustrated problem, some of the basic elements discussed in Chaps. 1 to 4. Consider the following problem: Surveying instruments (transit and theodolite), used for measuring angles, are calibrated in degrees, minutes, and seconds. Computer computations involving angular measurement require that the angle be expressed in radians. Write a FORTRAN program which will read from a data card the value of an angle in degrees, minutes, and seconds and which will calculate and print the value of that angle in decimal degrees and radians. The test data used is shown as a part of the printout.

Figure 4-10 shows a program that will accomplish the desired calculations. Note the liberal use of comment cards to explain successive steps and the use of the form of the READ statement discussed in Sec. 4-8. A careful review of the last three programs will illustrate and review many of the discussions in these first four chapters.

PROBLEMS

4-1
Revise Prob. 2-7 so as to handle any number of different boxes.

4-2
Revise Prob. 3-3 so as to handle any number of temperature values in degrees Celsius.

4-3
Write a program to read in any three values representing three lengths and determine if they can form a triangle; if they can, determine whether the triangle is a right triangle. Appropriate messages should then be printed, together with the values of each of the three sides.

4-4
Write a program to sum the values of the odd integers between 1 and 100.

4-5
Values for 10 sets of 3 variables each are to be read from data cards. The values must be arranged in order of descending magnitude on the data cards. Test the data for proper arrangement. If properly arranged, compute the sum of the three variables and print the values of the variables and their sum. If the data are not properly arranged, print the three variables and an appropriate message.

4-6
The values of E are defined as the limit of $(1 + X)^{1/x}$ as X approaches zero. Starting with $X = 2$ and decreasing X by one-half for each trial, determine the approximate value of E until the result is correct to five decimal places: $E = 2.71828$. Print each X and approximation of E.

PLANNING 5.
YOUR PROGRAM

5-1
INTRODUCTION

Too often, programmers, both beginners and those who should know better, simply start writing the program with little or no prior planning. The test results of these programs frequently turn out to be meaningless numbers (garbage) even though no compilation or execution errors are evident. Then long hours are spent in attempting to find the errors in the logic, errors which could have been avoided by advance planning.

This is a wasteful use of both the programmer's and the computer's time. Time costs money, and so a waste of time is also a waste of money. Some of this lost time and money would be saved if the programmer first sat down with a pencil, paper, and an eraser and tried to plan the most logical sequence to achieve the desired results. The most common system used in program planning is to construct a graphical diagram of the program using distinctly recognizable symbols for the various computer operations.

5-2
FLOW-DIAGRAM SYMBOLS

Although some standardization has been attempted, there is no universally accepted standard symbols to use in representing computer operations. Different texts and manuals about computers show some variations. The main concern in adopting a set of symbols is to have each symbol uniquely different so that it can be seen at a glance what is being done in the program.

The symbols used in this text are shown in Fig. 5-1. Stringing these symbols together with lines representing the flow of information and arrows showing the direction of flow creates a picture of the sequence of operations

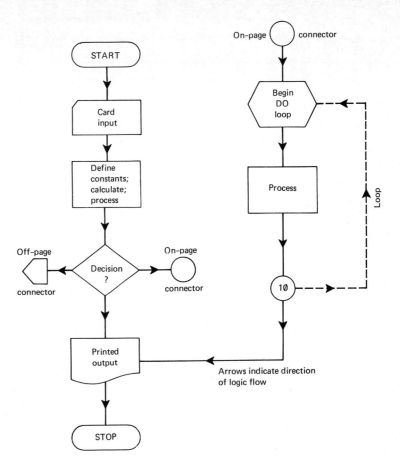

FIG. 5-1
Flow-diagram symbols.

in a program. The picture is called a *flow diagram*. Usually the flow diagram is at first roughly sketched by the programmer. Then as the flow diagram is studied, any logic errors that may occur can be seen and corrected or more efficient sequences can be discovered. This is why an eraser is so necessary in the creative phase of flow diagramming. After deciding upon the final arrangement, the best practice calls for making a neat drawing of the flow diagram, using a symbol template to outline the various operation symbols.

5-3
SAMPLE FLOW DIAGRAMS
The best way to understand the proper use of the symbols shown in Fig. 5-1 is to examine some examples of flow diagrams. Figure 5-2 shows the flow diagram of the circle problem using the DO statement, as discussed in Sec. 4-7. Solid lines represent the direct flow of operations. Dashed lines represent the transfer of control because of the DO statement. An examination of Fig. 5-2 gives the reader an understandable visual picture of the sequence, or logic, of the program.

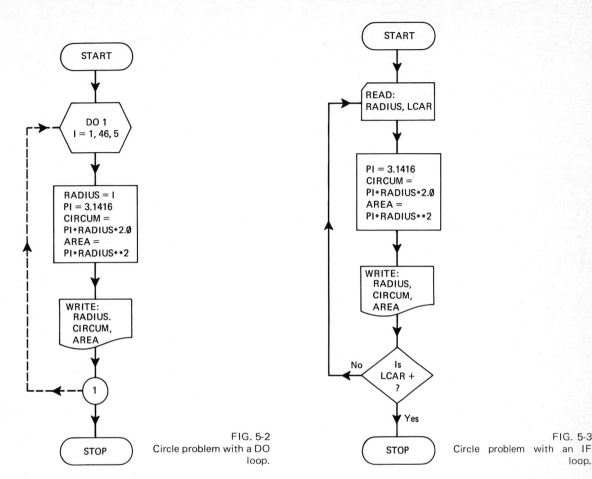

FIG. 5-2
Circle problem with a DO loop.

FIG. 5-3
Circle problem with an IF loop.

Figure 5-3 shows the same problem using an IF statement. Solid lines are used for the transfer of the control because the transfer is a direct result of a decision and also they visually differentiate between a DO loop and an IF loop.

Figure 5-4 shows the flow diagram of a problem to be discussed in detail in Chap. 11. We present it here to illustrate a more complicated problem and three more points: The first point is how to represent an unconditional GO TO statement. Note the arrows going from the symbol for the assignment statement X=X+DELTA and leading to the upper assignment symbol. This represents an unconditional GO TO following X=X+DELTA and transferring control to the first statement in the indicated assignment symbol. There are also unconditional GO TO statements following the two rightmost assignment symbols, transferring control to the same statement as the previous GO TO.

The second point is that when the programmer feels that it is advisable to indicate statement numbers, they can be shown as illustrated; for example, the READ statement is statement number 1. The last point is that a sketch can be included with the flow diagram to clarify an obscure concept that might not

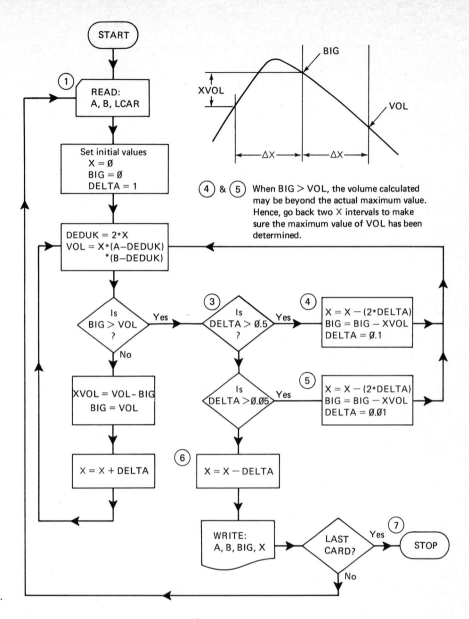

FIG. 5-4
Maximum volume problem.

be immediately apparent to the reader; such a sketch is shown in the upper right of Fig. 5-4.

5-4
DOCUMENTATION

Every programmer who has prepared a number of programs has had the experience of going back to a program written some time before and wondering why some particular operation or sequence was used. This problem can be avoided by a practice called *documentation*. The liberal use of comment cards and a well-drawn flow diagram are the first two essentials of documentation.

A written discussion of the program provides the final element. The objective should be to document the program so that any other person can read the program statements and documentation and understand what was done and why. Fig. 4-10 is an example of documentation by comment cards.

PROBLEMS
5-1
Prepare flow diagram for

a Prob. 4-1
b Prob. 4-3
c Prob. 4-5

5-2
Prepare a flow diagram showing how to determine if any integer value is odd or even.

5-3
The value of e^x may be approximated by iteration of the formula

$$e^x = 1 + \sum_{i=1}^{N} \frac{x^i}{i!}$$

Prepare a flow diagram showing how to determine the value of e^x for any x, with the number of iterations desired by the programmer.

5-4
Prepare a flow diagram that will compute and print the factorials of integers from 1 to 10 and will finally print out the summation of all factorials.

5-5
Prepare a flow diagram that will read any desired number of data cards, each containing one value, and sum the positive values, sum the negative values, and print both sums after all cards have been read.

WHAT 6. CALCULATIONS CAN FORTRAN DO FOR YOU?

6-1
INTRODUCTION

Computers are used because they can perform numerical operations and mathematical calculations very rapidly, reducing human time and effort and virtually eliminating human arithmetic errors in solving problems. Many mathematical calculations appear repeatedly in a variety of problems, for example, extracting the square root. The most common of these calculations are included in the FORTRAN system as "preprogrammed packages" known as *library functions*. Some of the most commonly used library functions will be described in this chapter. Others are given in Table A-4.

The number of library functions available depends on the type and model of computer used and on the unique requirements at each installation. Some installations, or computer centers, find that their programmers often use some special-purpose function and will build that function into the system. Therefore, each programmer must check with the local computer center to ascertain which library functions are available.

6-2
SQUARE ROOT

The square root of some value or expression is a common calculation. For the programmer to include the necessary arithmetic statements within each program to calculate the square root would require considerable time and knowledge. However, it is available in FORTRAN simply by writing

SQRT(a)

where a is a real value, variable, or expression. Some examples of the use of this function in arithmetic assignment statements are

Y=SQRT(ABLE)
DISCR=SQRT(B**2—4.*A*B)

In the first example, the computer (with no further instructions) will determine the square root of the value assigned to the variable ABLE and assign its value to the variable Y. In the second example, the computer will first evaluate the expression within the parentheses and then determine its square root and assign its value to DISCR.

6-3
ABSOLUTE VALUE
The use of the square-root function can lead to unexpected troubles for the beginner. The computer will not take the square root of a negative value, and if this situation arises, the computer usually rejects the program with an execution error. This situation can be avoided with the *absolute function*. This function does exactly what its name implies: It disregards the algebraic sign and deals with the absolute value. The general form of this function is

ABS(*a*)
IABS(*k*)

where *a* is a real value, variable, or expression and *k* is an integer value, variable, or expression. Examples of its use are

Y=ABS(ABLE)
Y=SQRT(ABS(ABLE))
I=IABS(NUMBR)

What is accomplished in the first example is obvious. In the second example, first the absolute value of ABLE is set and then its square root determined and assigned to the variable Y. This avoids the problem encountered if the value of ABLE is negative. The last example is the same as the first except that the values involved are integers.

6-4
EXPONENTIAL
In many scientific equations the value *e* (2.71828. . .) must be raised to some power. When the calculation is done by the programmer, the value of *e* must be defined and the number of decimal places established. This can be avoided by the use of the exponential function. The general form is

EXP(*a*)

where *a* can be a real value, variable, or expression. It means that *e* is raised to the *a* power. An example is

Y = ZEBRA*EXP(ABLE)

Here *e* is raised to the ABLE power and the result is multiplied by the value of ZEBRA and assigned to the variable Y.

6-5
LOGARITHMS

A rather complicated program for the beginner to write is a program to determine the logarithm of a number. Two functions are used to determine logarithms:

ALOG(*a*)
ALOG1Ø(*a*)

The first function determines the natural logarithm of *a,* and the second determines the common logarithm of *a.* Examples of their use are

Y=ALOG(ABLE)
Y=EXP(ALOG1Ø(ABLE))

In the first statement, the value of the natural log of the value of ABLE is assigned to Y. In the second, the value of *e* raised to the power whose value is the common logarithm of the value of ABLE is assigned to Y.

6-6
SINE AND COSINE

When the sine or cosine of some angle is required, the sine or cosine function will provide that value. The general form is

SIN(*a*)
COS(*a*)

The value of the angle (*a*) must be in radians. Any value that is in degrees or other angular units must first be converted to radians. Examples of the use of sine and cosine functions are

Y=SIN(ADEG*3.14159/18Ø.)
SIN2A=2.Ø*SIN(ARAD)*COS(ARAD)

In the first example, the sine of ADEG is determined with the value of ADEG expressed in degrees; the result is assigned to Y. The second example is the computerized version of the familiar equation for the sine of 2 times an angle. The value of the variable ARAD must be expressed in radians for use in this statement.

Note that no library function is included for calculating the tangent of an angle. The tangent can be determined using the trigonometric relationship: tan = sin/cos, or as expressed in FORTRAN; TANA = SIN(A)/COS(A). The variable TANA is not a function.

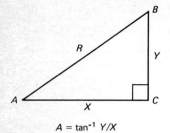

$A = \tan^{-1} Y/X$

FIG. 6-1
Right-triangle relationship.

6-7
ARCTANGENT

A common trigonometric application is determining the size of an angle from its tangent. The arctangent function serves this purpose. The general form is

ATAN(*t*)

where (*t*) is the tangent of a given angle. An example of the use of the arctangent function is

A = ATAN(Y/X)

where in a right triangle Y is the value of the opposite side and X is the value of the adjacent side. The value in radians of the angle defined is assigned to the variable A. See Fig. 6-1.

6-8
ARGUMENT OF THE FUNCTION

The variable or expression enclosed in parentheses is called the *argument* of the function and must always be a real value except for the function: IABS(*k*). When the argument represents the size of an angle, the value must be expressed in radians.

PROBLEMS
6-1

Write a program to compute the roots of any quadratic equation. The program must be able to handle the case of complex roots.

6-2
Compute the following functions of N: N^2, $\sqrt{N}$, N^3, $\sqrt[3]{N}$, and $1/N$. Start with $N = 2$ and end when $\sqrt{N} = 2\sqrt[3]{N}$. Increment N in steps of 2.

6-3
Calculate and print a table showing the sine, cosine, and tangent of angles from $\emptyset$ to $90°$ in increments of $5°$. Explain what occurs for the value of the tangent of $9\emptyset°$.

6-4
Revise Prob. 3-5 to compute the size of the three angles in degrees. Remember that the cosine of angle C is negative, and write a program so that the correct value in degrees is computed. Make the program such that it will handle the conditions if any three sides of a triangle are read in. Test the program with data for at least three triangles. Also remember that the cosine of $9\emptyset°$ is zero. Write your program to avoid division by zero.

LOGICAL 7. DECISIONS

7-1
INTRODUCTION

Chapter 4 introduced the arithmetic IF statement and discussed how it is used to transfer control to a given statement based on the numeric value or algebraic sign of a test arithmetic expression. A second and perhaps more useful transfer statement is the logical IF. The logical IF statement employs logical expressions and relational operators and makes decisions based on the relationship between two or more arithmetic expressions. Some programming experience is necessary to fully appreciate the power of the logical IF.

7-2
LOGICAL EXPRESSIONS AND RELATIONAL OPERATORS

A *logical expression* is one that asks a question about two or more arithmetic expressions: Is A less than B? Is C greater than D? Is E equal to F? The following six basic *relational operators* are used to ask such relational questions:

Relational Operator	Meaning
.LT.	less than
.LE.	less than or equal to
.EQ.	equal to
.GE.	greater than or equal to
.GT.	greater than
.NE.	not equal to

The periods are necessary parts of the operator. Using these relational operators to make a logical expression, we could say:

Logical Expression	Meaning
A.LT.B	Is A less than B?
C.EQ.(D/E)	Is C equal to D divided by E?
X.GT.(R+S)	Is X greater than R plus S?

In the last two expressions the parentheses are necessary to clearly show that the comparison called for by the relational operator applies to the entire value within the parentheses.

Two other relational operators greatly extend the usefulness of a logical expression: .AND. and .OR. An example of the .AND. operator is

A.LT.B.AND.C.GT.D

This expression asks: Is A less than B *and* is C greater than D? The .AND. requires that *both* conditions be satisfied for the expression to be true. An example of an .OR. operator is

E.GE.F.OR.G.LE.(H−X)

This expression asks: Is E greater than or equal to F or is G less than or equal to the value of H minus X? The .OR. means that when *either* condition is true, the expression is true.

All logical expressions are either true or false. In the expression A.LT.B, if A is less than B, the expression is true; but if A is equal to or greater than B, the expression is false.

7-3
THE LOGICAL IF STATEMENT
The general form of the logical IF statement is

IF(logic)statement

where "logic" is a logical expression and "statement" is any executable FORTRAN statement other than another logical IF or a DO statement. The execution of the logical IF statement is as follows:

1 The logical expression is evaluated as being either true or false.

2 If the expression is true, the statement is executed. If the statement is an arithmetic IF or a GO TO statement, control is transferred as indicated. If the statement is an arithmetic assignment statement (or any other executable statement), that statement is executed and the program continues in sequence with the statement immediately following the logical IF statement.

3 If the expression is false, no action results and the program continues in sequence with the statement immediately following the logical IF statement.

Note that whether the expression is true or false the statement immediately following the logical IF statement is always executed unless the statement is an arithmetic IF or GO TO and the logical expression is true. Some examples of logical IF statements and discussions of what happens are now given.

Suppose that when I is greater than 2, Y is equal to X to the power of I; but when I is equal to or less than 2, Y is equal to X to the power of 2 times I. In all cases, W is equal to T/Y. These conditions can be met with the following statements:

```
IF(I.GT.2)Y=X**I
IF(I.LE.2)Y=X**(I*2)
W=T/Y
```

When the first IF statement is encountered, if I is greater than 2, the statement Y=X**I will be executed. Then control passes to the second IF statement. Since the expression in the first IF statement is true, then the expression in the second IF statement must be false. Therefore, control is passed to the third statement, and the value of the expression T/(X**I) will be assigned to W.

On the other hand, if the expression encountered in the first IF statement is false, control will be passed to the second IF statement. Since the expression in the first IF statement is false, the expression in the second IF statement must be true and the statement Y = X**(I*2) will be executed. Then control would pass to the third statement, and the value of the expression T/(X**(I*2)) will be assigned to W. Thus, different values of Y are calculated for the two stated conditions.

The student might wonder if two IF statements are needed. Since if I is not greater than 2, then Y must be X**(I*2), could not the same result have been reached by

```
IF(I.GT.2)Y=X**I
Y=X**(I*2)
W=T/Y
```

Examine the statements: If I is greater than 2, then Y = X**I. But then control is passed to the statement immediately following the IF statement, and Y is recalculated as Y = X**(I*2). If I is not greater than 2, control is passed to the next statement and Y = X**(I*2). In other words, no matter what the value of I, Y will always be the same. Therefore, the preceding statements do not satisfy the given conditions.

For another example, consider these conditions: DELTA is assigned an initial value of 1.Ø. After a series of calculations, it is desired to reset DELTA to a value of Ø.1 and repeat the calculations. After this sequence, it is desired again to reset DELTA to a value of Ø.Ø1 and repeat the calculations. No further changes in the value of DELTA are to be made. These requirements can be met by the following instructions, where statement 2 starts the desired calculations:

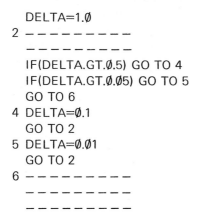

```
  DELTA=1.Ø
2 ─ ─ ─ ─ ─ ─ ─ ─
  ─ ─ ─ ─ ─ ─ ─ ─
  IF(DELTA.GT.Ø.5) GO TO 4
  IF(DELTA.GT.Ø.Ø5) GO TO 5
  GO TO 6
4 DELTA=Ø.1
  GO TO 2
5 DELTA=Ø.Ø1
  GO TO 2
6 ─ ─ ─ ─ ─ ─ ─ ─
  ─ ─ ─ ─ ─ ─ ─ ─
  ─ ─ ─ ─ ─ ─ ─ ─
```

When the first IF is encountered, DELTA is 1.Ø and hence greater than Ø.5. Therefore, control will be transferred to statement number 4 where DELTA is reset to Ø.1. Then control is transferred to statement number 2 at the beginning of the calculation. When the first IF is again encountered, DELTA is not greater than Ø.5 and so control is passed to the second IF statement. DELTA is greater than Ø.Ø5, and therefore control will be transferred to statement number 5 where DELTA is reset to Ø.Ø1. Control then is transferred to statement number 2. When the first IF is encountered again, DELTA is not greater than Ø.5 and so control passes to the second IF statement. Here DELTA is not greater than Ø.Ø5 and so control passes to the next statement, which transfers control to statement number 6, and the remainder of the program can be completed. The preceding example illustrates the use of, not only the logical IF statement, but also the unconditional GO TO first described in Sec. 4-2.

PROBLEMS
7-1
Write a program that will compute the reactions, bending moments, and deflections for a simple beam with a single concentrated load. (Refer to an appropriate engineering handbook for necessary definitions and mathematical formulas.) The input should include the load, the span of the beam and the position of the load, the modulus of elasticity of the beam, its moment of inertia, and the interval at which it is desired to calculate bending moments. (This interval should be some whole number that is a multiple of the span.) The output should include the initial data for the beam, the values of the two reactions, and a table showing the bending moment and deflection at each

interval across the beam. The maximum moment and its deflection should also be shown. The program should be able to handle as many beams as desired.

7-2
Any previous problem requiring decisions may be assigned.

WHEN A VARIABLE NEEDS MORE THAN ONE VALUE

8.

8-1
INTRODUCTION

It is often necessary to work with quantities which are elements of an associated group called an *array*. An array is a complete set of quantities, all of which have the same variable name. Consider the solution of three simultaneous equations involving three unknown variables: Three different coefficients of X, three different coefficients of Y, three different coefficients of Z, and three different answer values are involved. Of course, each coefficient and answer could be assigned to a different variable name, but then there would be the problem of locating the position of each variable as the program to solve the equations is being written. It greatly simplifies matters to refer to all the coefficients of each unknown as elements of an array. This chapter will discuss arrays as defined in FORTRAN and some of the statements associated with arrays.

8-2
ARRAYS

Arrays in FORTRAN may be one-, two-, or three-dimensional. Larger arrays are sometimes permitted but are rarely needed. A one-dimensional array can be established from a list of associated values such as the number of cars passing through a traffic light when the light is green. The array might be 33, 37, 34, 20, 29, 10 for successive cycles of the light.

A two-dimensional array involves two related elements such as a sales record showing the number of cars of various makes that are sold in different cities each month. Figure 8-1 shows such an array.

In mathematical notation, a one-dimensional array can be written as

$$x_1, x_2, x_3, x_4, x_5, \ldots, x_n$$

	Car A	Car B	Car C	Car D
New York	800	500	1200	303
Chicago	750	620	833	425
Cleveland	600	720	756	555

FIG. 8-1
A two-dimensional array.

where the numerals 1, 2, 3, 4, and 5 are known as subscripts. The card punch used in preparing computer cards cannot punch a subscript character in the position shown in the mathematical notation. Hence, in FORTRAN, this array would be written

X(1), X(2), X(3), X(4), X(5), . . . , X(N)

In mathematical notation, the array shown in Fig. 8-1 could be written as

$$n_{1,1}\ n_{1,2}\ n_{1,3}\ n_{1,4}$$
$$n_{2,1}\ n_{2,2}\ n_{2,3}\ n_{2,4}$$
$$n_{3,1}\ n_{3,2}\ n_{3,3}\ n_{3,4}$$

In FORTRAN the same array becomes

	Col. 1	Col. 2	Col. 3	Col. 4
Row 1	N(1,1)	N(1,2)	N(1,3)	N(1,4)
Row 2	N(2,1)	N(2,2)	N(2,3)	N(2,4)
Row 3	N(3,1)	N(3,2)	N(3,3)	N(3,4)

The variables named X and N with subscripts X(1) and N(1,1) are known as *subscripted variables*. Since larger arrays (more than two subscripts) have only special applications, discussion will be limited to the two types of arrays shown previously.

In FORTRAN, a subscripted variable can be either integer- or real-mode. The variable name follows the same rules as those for the name of a nonsubscripted variable. Since the same variable name is used for all elements of the array, it is apparent that values of the elements cannot be mixed in mode. Values must be either all integer values or all real values. Subscripts must always be integer numbers. Zero is not acceptable as a subscript.

By examining the preceding arrays, it can be seen that when a single subscript is used (a one-dimensional array), it identifies the position of a particular element in the row of the array. For example, X(4) is the fourth element in the array X(N). When two subscripts are used (a two-dimensional array), the first subscript identifies the row and the second identifies the column of the array. Thus, N(2,3) is in the second row and the third column of that array.

The rules of FORTRAN allow the following forms of subscripts, where I and J are integer constants and M is an integer variable:

Subscript Form	Meaning Subscript Is a
I	Constant
M	Variable
M+I or M−I	Variable plus a constant or variable minus a constant
I*M	Constant times a variable
I*M+J or I*M−J	Constant times a variable plus a constant or constant times a variable minus a constant

Some examples of allowable subscripted variables are N(3), N(I), A(IX), B(2,J), ABLE(N+1,K), INTER(2*L,I+3), and XRAY(3,3*M+4). No other forms of subscripts are allowable. For example, the subscript arrangement in ABLE(3+N) is not allowed while ABLE(N+3) is permissible.

Since an integer variable can be used as a subscript or as part of the subscript, the unique value of any subscripted variable in an array can be identified if the value of the subscript variable has been defined previously in the program. This makes possible any desired manipulation or calculations involving arrays and will be demonstrated in the examples given in Secs. 8-6 and 8-7.

8-3
THE DIMENSION STATEMENT

The use of subscripted variables can create some confusion in the computer. When the variable name X is first encountered, one location in storage must be reserved for the value of X. But when the subscripted variable name X(N) first appears, the number of storage locations, or words, to reserve for this variable is unknown. Hence, when subscripted variables are used, certain information must be supplied to the computer at the very beginning of the program. This information is provided by a statement identifying the

1 Variable names that are subscripted

2 Number of subscripts used (one- or two-dimensional)

3 Maximum integer value that each subscript may have

The DIMENSION statement provides this information and, therefore, must appear in the program before the computer encounters the first subscripted variable. A DIMENSION statement, since it requires no calculations or decisions, is a nonexecutable statement. The customary place for the DIMENSION statement to appear is at the beginning of the program before any executable statement. The general form of the DIMENSION statement is

DIMENSION A(5), B(1Ø,15),...,N(1ØØ,5)

where A, B, and N represent the subscripted variable names followed by parentheses containing the maximum integer value of the subscript. If there are two subscripts, their maximum values are separated by a comma. An example of a DIMENSION statement is

DIMENSION CAN(3Ø), ZIP(1Ø,5)

Here there are two subscripted variables named CAN and ZIP within the program. CAN is one-dimensional, while ZIP is two-dimensional; both are real-mode. The computer will assign 3Ø storage locations to the variable CAN and 5Ø (1Ø X 5) locations to the variable ZIP. Knowing this, the computer will automatically place each individual value of each array in its proper storage location so that when a programmer uses CAN(3), it is certain that neither CAN(2), CAN(4), nor any other value of CAN will be obtained. It is important to distinguish between the value assigned to a given subscripted variable name and its position in the array as described by the subscripts.

8-4
READING SUBSCRIPTED VALUES INTO THE COMPUTER

Reading subscripted values for storage within the computer complicates the programmer's task because the programmer must ensure that the values are read in the proper order. Consider a one-dimensional array named X which contains five values. One way in which the values can be read is

```
    DIMENSION X(5)
    DO 1 I=1,5
  1 READ(1,1ØØ) X(I)
1ØØ FORMAT(F1Ø.5)
```

The computer will reserve five locations, as specified in the DIMENSION statement, for the five anticipated values of X, each identified by integer subscripts X(1), X(2), X(3), X(4), and X(5). Under the control of the DO loop, the value of subscript variable I is incremented from 1 to 5 and one value is read from each of five data cards and assigned successively to X(1), X(2), X(3), X(4), and X(5). If the data cards get out of order, the computer will still read and store values in successive locations but with unpredictable results.

Putting all five values on the same data card and changing the FORMAT statement to FORMAT(5F1Ø.5) will not work because the READ statement lists only one variable. When one value is read and assigned to that variable, execution is completed. The next time the READ statement is reached in the loop, the computer will read a new card which will not contain the desired value or terminate the program if no more data cards remain. But the loop can be rewritten as

```
    DIMENSION X(5)
    READ(1,1ØØ) X(1), X(2), X(3), X(4), X(5)
1ØØ FORMAT(5F1Ø.5)
```

which will cause the five successive values of X to be read from the same card. However, if the array is large, using this method will require a lengthy READ statement. Another way of writing the READ statement can be used, utilizing an *implied* DO loop. The statements now become

```
    DIMENSION X(5)
    READ(1,100) (X(N),N=1,5)
100 FORMAT(5F10.5)
```

which will cause the computer to read the five successive values of X from the same card while the subscript variable increments from 1 to 5.

Now consider reading a two-dimensional array. Suppose that a 3 X 4 array (3 rows of 4 columns) similar to that of Fig. 8-1 is to be read. This reading can be accomplished with the following statements:

```
    DIMENSION X(3,4)
    DO 1 I=1,3
    DO 1 J=1,4
  1 READ(1,100) X(I,J)
100 FORMAT(F10.5)
```

In executing this double loop, the index of the outer loop (I) will first be set to 1. Then the index of the inner loop (J) will be set to 1, and the value of X(1,1) will be read. Then the index of the inner loop will be changed to 2, and the value of X(1,2) will be read, and so on through the value of X(1,4). When the inner loop has been satisfied, the index of the outer loop will be incremented to 2 and since the inner loop is starting all over, the index of the inner loop will be reset to 1 and the value X(2,1) is read. This process is repeated until all 12 values are read. Twelve data cards are required with one value per card.

Another way in which the data can be read is

```
    DIMENSION X(3,4)
    DO 1 I=1,3
    READ(1,100) (X(I,J),J=1,4)
100 FORMAT(4F10.5)
```

In this sequence, the index of the DO loop is set at 1 and the READ statement will read the four values in each row under the control of the implied DO loop. This process requires the use of three data cards (one card for each row), each containing four values (one value for each column). Still another way in which this array can be read is

```
    DIMENSION X(3,4)
    READ(1,100) ((X(I,J),J=1,4),I=1,3)
100 FORMAT(4F10.5)
```

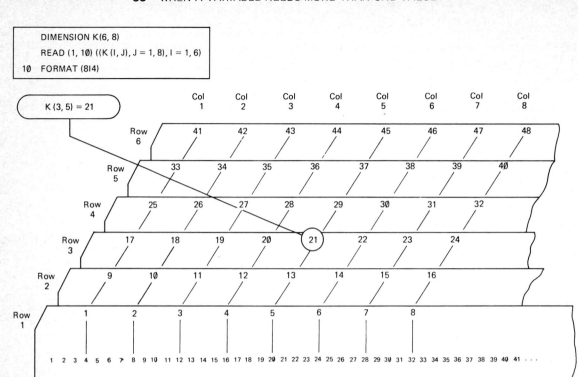

FIG. 8-2
Reading an array with an implied DO loop.

which is a *double implied* DO loop. Within the outer parentheses, I will be set at 1; then within the inner parentheses, J will vary from 1 to 4, reading the four values in the first row. Then within the outer parentheses, I will be changed to 2; and within the inner parentheses, J will again vary from 1 to 4, reading the four values of the second row. Similarly the values in the third row will be read. This method still requires the use of three data cards since the FORMAT specification allows only four values. Figure 8-2 illustrates the statements needed and the data cards necessary to read a two-dimensional array with an implied DO loop.

The DIMENSION statement must specify the largest subscript value, not simply the number of values to be stored. For example, if a program requires the use of $X(1)$, $X(3)$, and $X(5)$, the DIMENSION statement must be DIMENSION $X(5)$. The use of DIMENSION $X(3)$ will result in a subscript error and termination of the program.

8-5
PRINTING SUBSCRIPTED VARIABLES
Preparing the WRITE statement for printing subscripted variables follows the same sequence as in reading subscripted variables. In all the following discus-

sions, it will be assumed that the DIMENSION statement is given in its proper place in the program before any executable statements.

The same one-dimensional array used in Sec. 8-4 can be printed by

```
    DO 5 I=1,5
  5 WRITE(3,100) X(I)
100 FORMAT(1X,F10.5)
```

This sequence will cause the array to be printed in a column rather than a row because as each subscripted variable is printed, the WRITE statement is satisfied and the paper is advanced one line.

If the array is to be printed in one row, as usual, the requirement can be met by either set of the following statements:

```
    WRITE(3,100) X(1), X(2), X(3), X(4), X(5)
100 FORMAT(1X,5F15.5)
```

or

```
    WRITE(3,100)(X(I),I=1,5)
100 FORMAT(1X,5F15.5)
```

The wider field in the FORMAT statement is intended to provide space between the values. The advantage of the method using the implied DO loop for larger arrays is obvious.

Instructions for printing the same two-dimensional arrays illustrated in Sec. 8-2 by the use of two nested DO loops are

```
    DO 10 I=1,3
    DO 10 J=1,4
 10 WRITE(3,100) N(I,J)
100 FORMAT(1X,I10)
```

This sequence will cause all 12 values in the array to be printed in one long column. There is no quick visual way of knowing in which row or column a particular value belongs.

Printing the array in its rows and columns can be accomplished by either set of the following statements:

```
    DO 10 I=1,3
    WRITE(3,100)(N(I,J),J=1,4)
100 FORMAT(1X,4I15)
```

or

```
    WRITE (3,100)((N(I,J),J=1,4),I=1,3)
100 FORMAT(1X,4I15)
```

```
DIMENSION K (6, 8)
   WRITE (3, 10) ((K (I, J), J = 1, 8), I = 1, 6)
10  FORMAT (8I4)
```

K (3, 5) = 21

	Col 1	Col 2	Col 3	Col 4	Col 5	Col 6	Col 7	Col 8
Row 1	1	2	3	4	5	6	7	8
Row 2	9	1 0	1 1	1 2	1 3	1 4	1 5	1 6
Row 3	1 7	1 8	1 9	2 0	(2 1)	2 2	2 3	2 4
Row 4	2 5	2 6	2 7	2 8	2 9	3 0	3 1	3 2
Row 5	3 3	3 4	3 5	3 6	3 7	3 8	3 9	4 0
Row 6	4 1	4 2	4 3	4 4	4 5	4 6	4 7	4 8

1 2 3 4 5 6 7 8 9 10 11 12 13 14 15 16 17 18 19 20 21 22 23 24 25 26 27 28 29 30 31 32 33 34 35 ···

Print column

FIG. 8-3
Printing an array with an implied DO loop.

Detailed discussions of the actions caused by the various sets of WRITE statements have not been given because they are similar to the discussions of the different sets of READ statements. Figure 8-3 illustrates the use of the implied DO loop in printing the array read in Fig. 8-2.

There are times when such a large amount of data is involved that the values cannot be printed on one line. There are several ways in which this situation can be handled, but the most common way is to control the printing by the FORMAT statement. Consider the following statement:

```
   WRITE(3,100)(VAR(I),I=1,200)
100  FORMAT(1X,10F10.6)
```

Here there are 200 items of data to print. Obviously, they cannot be printed on one line, and the FORMAT statement accounts for only 10 values. The computer will cause the first 10 values to be printed according to the FORMAT statement. Then the specifications of the FORMAT are completed, but the WRITE statement still calls for more printing. Therefore the computer will start over again on the FORMAT statement, printing the next 10 values on the next line, and this cycle will be repeated until the demands of the WRITE statement are satisfied. The result in this case is a 20 X 10 array of values. An example can be seen in Fig. 11-1.

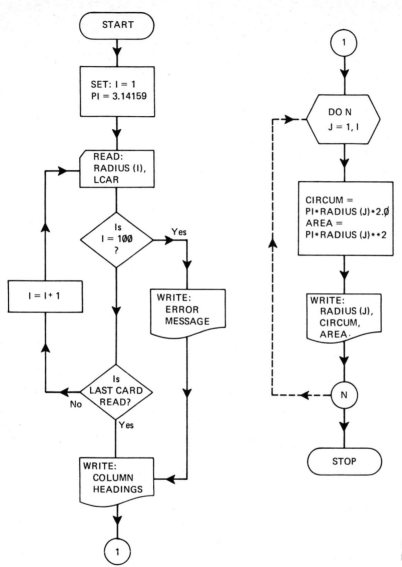

FIG. 8-4
Flow diagram of the circle problem using subscripted variables.

8-6
FIRST EXAMPLE

The circle problem shown previously in Sec. 4-7 and Figs. 4-8 and 4-9 can be revised to demonstrate some interesting points. Since the use of subscripted variables requires a decision as to the maximum number of subscripts, the number of circles calculated in any one program run will be limited arbitrarily to 100. (This means that the program must be rerun with different data cards if more than 100 circles are involved.)

The first step is to develop the flow diagram (Fig. 8-4) for the solution. The variable I will be a counter to count the number of cards read. Since it is not known how many data cards containing values of the radius are to be read, initiate the first value of I as I=1. The value of π, PI=3.14159, must also be defined. Next read the first value of the radius: RADIUS (I). (This shows why the value of I must be set initially at 1 rather than 0. Zero is an unacceptable subscript. Therefore, even though no cards have then been read, the initial value of the counter I must be set at 1 because I is also used as a subscript.) Since RADIUS is a subscripted variable and the maximum number of subscripts has been defined, a protective check must be made to ensure that the maximum number is not exceeded. Therefore, immediately after each card has been read, a check must be made to see if 100 cards (I=100?) have been read. If so, an appropriate warning message can be programmed and a transfer can be made to some subsequent statement in the program.

Next another check must be made to see if the last data card has been read. If not, the value of I must be incremented by 1 and the next card read. If the last card has been read, calculations can begin. In this example, column headings to identify output values are used and so at this time the column headings should be printed. It is also to this point that the transfer from the protective check should be made.

All the calculations and printing can be accomplished under the control of a DO statement where the index J varies from a value of 1 to a value of I since the value of I is the number of cards read. After the DO loop is completed, the problem is finished. The completed flow diagram of this problem is shown in Fig. 8-4. Note the use of the junction symbol marked 1. As the flow diagram was drawn, it could be seen that it would be quite long. To conserve vertical space, the left portion was ended using this junction symbol. Then the flow diagram was resumed to the right of the first part, first using the same junction symbol, thus showing that the right portion of the flow diagram is a continuation of the left portion. Note also the circle with an N inside at the end of the range of the DO loop. Since the statement numbers are not known, the proper statement number can not be put in at this time. This is unimportant, however, for the purpose of the flow diagram is to show the flow of information.

Now the statements of the program can be written. The program and its results are shown in Fig. 8-5.

8-7
ANOTHER EXAMPLE PROBLEM

A teacher requests a program to help her study grades. She assures you that there will always be just 25 grades. Since tests are turned in at random during the period, there is no set order of papers. The papers are graded in the order turned in. The teacher will provide a list of grades in that order. She wants a listing of the grades in numerical order and the average of the grades. How can this be accomplished?

Since the teacher says that there will always be 25 grades, it is decided to read the grades with an integer subscripted variable IGRADE(I) using an implied DO loop. After the grades are read, it is necessary to rearrange them in numerical order. For this purpose another variable is needed, called JGRADE(I). If a variable called IBIG is set up within the DO loop, all grades

```
 1              DATA ICR,IPR/1,3/
 2              DIMENSION RADIUS(100)
 3              I=1
 4              PI=3.14159
 5            1 READ(ICR,100) RADIUS(I),LCAR
 6          100 FORMAT(F10.3,I4)
 7              IF(I.EQ.100)GO TO 3
 8              IF(LCAR)2,2,4
 9            2 I=I+1
10              GO TO 1
11            3 WRITE(IPR,200)
12          200 FORMAT(1X,'ERROR - READING HAS BEEN HALTED SINCE 100 CARDS HAVE BE
               1EN READ',///)
13            4 WRITE(IPR,300)
14          300 FORMAT(10X,'RADIUS',5X,'CIRCUMFERENCE',6X,'AREA',/)
15              DO 5 J=1,I
16              CIRCUM=PI*RADIUS(J)*2.0
17              AREA=PI*RADIUS(J)**2
18            5 WRITE(IPR,400)RADIUS(J),CIRCUM,AREA
19          400 FORMAT(1X,3F15.3,/)
20              STOP
21              END
```

RADIUS	CIRCUMFERENCE	AREA
1.000	6.283	3.142
2.500	15.708	19.635
4.750	29.845	70.882
7.255	45.584	165.358
10.333	64.924	335.430
12.000	75.398	452.389
15.000	94.248	706.858
25.782	161.993	2088.250
55.000	345.575	9503.309
125.000	785.397	49087.340

FIG. 8-5
Circle problem with sub-
scripted variables.

can be compared with that variable. For the first comparison, the variable IBIG is always assigned the value of the first grade. Thus, IBIG is set equal to IGRADE(1). Then, using an inner DO loop (Fig. 8-6), IBIG can be compared with the remaining IGRADEs. If IBIG is greater than the next IGRADE, nothing is done but to continue the comparison. But if IBIG is not greater than the next IGRADE, a new value for IBIG is assigned equal to that value of IGRADE. When the inner loop is satisfied, IBIG will always be the largest value compared and the first value of JGRADE will be the value of IBIG.

Since the sum of the grades is needed, they can be added and the sum assigned to a variable called ITOT. However, before the start of the DO loops an initial value for ITOT must be assigned: ITOT=0. Now consider the second time through the outer loop. If the values of the various IGRADEs remain unchanged, IBIG will always have the same value. Therefore, the largest value of IGRADE must be eliminated each time the inner loop is completed. This can be done by putting a variable (N) in the inner loop which will always contain the value of the subscript of the largest value of IGRADE. Then when the inner loop is completed, that value of IGRADE can be set to zero so that it will not be the biggest value the next time through the inner loop.

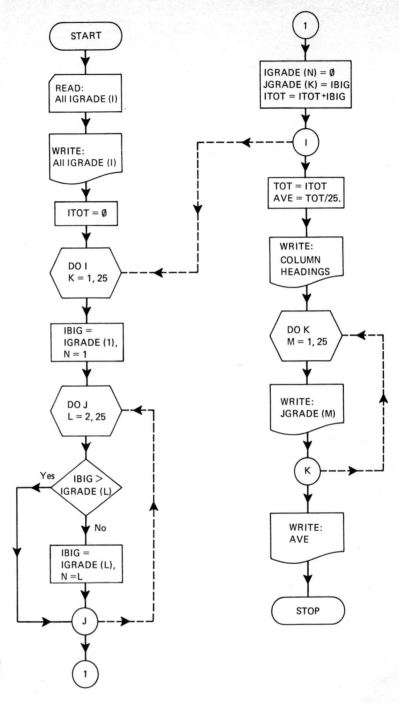

FIG. 8-6
Flow diagram of the grade problem using subscripted variables.

When the two nested DO loops are completed, the subscripted variable JGRADE will contain the grades in numerical order. Then the average grade can be calculated and column headings and results printed. It was decided to print the output in a column form because a teacher would be more accus-

```
          $JOB      NCS.FE.F1201/HAMMOND
          C FIGURE 8-7
     1          DATA ICR,IPR/1,3/
     2          DIMENSION IGRADE(25),JGRADE(25)
     3          READ(ICR,100)(IGRADE(I),I=1,25)
     4      100 FORMAT(25I3)
     5          WRITE(IPR,500)(IGRADE(I),I=1,25)
     6      500 FORMAT(2X,25I4,///)
     7          ITOT=0
     8          DO 2 K=1,25
     9          IBIG=IGRADE(1)
    10          N=1
    11          DO 1 L=2,25
    12          IF(IBIG.GT.IGRADE(L))GO TO 1
    13          IBIG=IGRADE(L)
    14          N=L
    15        1 CONTINUE
    16          IGRADE(N)=0
    17          JGRADE(K)=IBIG
    18        2 ITOT=ITOT+IBIG
    19          TOT=ITOT
    20          AVE=TOT/25.
    21          WRITE(IPR,200)
    22      200 FORMAT(4X,'ORDER OF GRADES',/)
    23          WRITE(IPR,300)(JGRADE(M),M=1,25)
    24      300 FORMAT(10X,I3)
    25          WRITE(IPR,400)AVE
    26      400 FORMAT(1X,'THE AVERAGE GRADE =',F6.2)
    27          STOP
    28          END
```

FIG. 8-7
Grade problem with sub-
scripted variables.

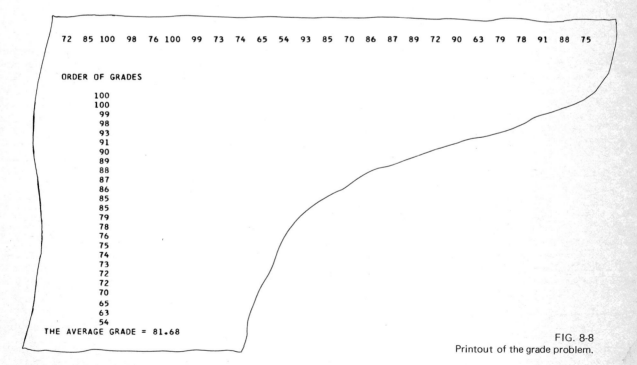

```
 72  85 100  98  76 100  99  73  74  65  54  93  85  70  86  87  89  72  90  63  79  78  91  88  75


ORDER OF GRADES

          100
          100
           99
           98
           93
           91
           90
           89
           88
           87
           86
           85
           85
           79
           78
           76
           75
           74
           73
           72
           72
           70
           65
           63
           54
THE AVERAGE GRADE = 81.68
```

FIG. 8-8
Printout of the grade problem.

tomed to seeing the data in that form. The completed flow diagram is shown in Fig. 8-6, and the resulting program is shown in Fig. 8-7. The printout is shown in Fig. 8-8 where the student can compare the original array with the final array.

PROBLEMS

8-1
Generate a multiplication table for numbers from 1 to 1Ø. Provide for row and column headings (number of row or column). *Hint*: Each value in the table will equal its row multiplied by its column.

8-2
Generate a table of volumes in gallons for right circular tanks whose radii vary from 1 to 1Ø ft in increments of 1 ft and whose heights vary from 1 to 9 ft in increments of 2 ft. Provide column headings and titles.

8-3
Write a program that will search an *N* X *M* matrix for the value of the largest element. The maximum matrix will be a 1Ø X 1Ø matrix. Have the matrix printed as well as its maximum element. The program should handle any number of matrices. Assume all values in the matrix are integers. Search through at least two different *N* X *M* matrices.

8-4
Write a program that will read any number of values up to 1ØØ values and keep count of the number read. When all the values have been read, calculate and print the average of the values read.

8-5
It is desired to design a dipstick to measure the number of gallons remaining in a cylindrical storage tank that is positioned with the length axis horizontal. The diameter of the tank is 1Ø ft, and the length of the tank is 2Ø ft. The dipstick should be marked as close as possible to increments of 2ØØ gal. Distances from the bottom of the dipstick to each graduation are to be determined to Ø.ØØ1 ft (Ø.Ø12 in). *Caution*: Be careful in calculating the volumes and distances for the upper half of the tank.

8-6
A ticket distribution office desires to computerize its operations to ensure that the correct amount is charged and the correct amount of change is returned to the customer either by mailing a check or in direct "over-the-counter" transaction. Write a program that will read-in the customer's name and address, number of tickets ordered, price of that particular ticket, and amount of money submitted with the order. Determine the total cost of the number of tickets ordered and the amount of refund due. The program should print special messages if no refund is due (be careful) or if insufficient money was submitted with the order. Then, if a refund is due, determine the number of dollars, half-dollars, quarters, dimes, nickles, and pennies in the refund (for the benefit of the clerks handling an over-the-counter transaction). The program should be able to handle any number of orders. Use test data that will test all options.

FINDING 9.
THE BUG

9-1
INTRODUCTION

So your program would not run! Well, friend, welcome to the club! The authors know of no programmers who always get their programs to run the first time, and some of the programs that do run either do not run to completion or do not give the expected results. In such cases the problem is to find out what went wrong, or to find the "bug" in the program. Computer people call this search for errors *debugging*.

There are three types of possible errors: compilation errors, execution errors, and logic errors. Compilation errors are most easily detected and corrected.

9-2
COMPILATION ERRORS

Every computer that has the capability of accepting programs written in FORTRAN IV (or any other computer language) can do so only because there is available a set of instructions telling the computer how to interpret the statements as written. This set of instructions is known as a *compiler program* (see Sec. 1-3). In addition to interpreting the statements, most compiler programs also are written to print error messages to point out various common and predictable mistakes. The compiler used for the programs presented in this text is known as WATFIV (the fifth version of a compiler program originating at Waterloo University in Canada). The illustrations in this chapter show examples of some of its messages. (Students should not expect identical messages for the same errors at their own computer centers. They should find out what error messages are used at their local installations and how to interpret them.)

```
     1              DATA ICR,IPR/1,3/
     2              READ(ICR,100)A,B,C
     3              FORMAT(3F10.4)
**WARNING**    NO STATEMENT NUMBER ON FORMAT STATEMENT
     4              DISC=SQRT(B**2-4.*/A*C)
***ERROR***    ILLEGAL SEQUENCE OF OPERATORS IN EXPRESSION
     5              ROOT1=(-B+DISC)/(2.*A
***ERROR***    UNMATCHED PARENTHESIS
     6              ROOT2=(-B-DISC)/(2.*A)
                    WRITE(IPR,200)ROOT1,ROOT2
***ERROR***    UNDECODEABLE STATEMENT
     7              IF(LCAR)1,1,7
     8           7 STOP
     9              END
***ERROR***    MISSING FORMAT STATEMENT      100 USED IN LINE      2
***ERROR***    MISSING STATEMENT NUMBER        1 USED IN LINE      7
```

FIG. 9-1
Typical compilation errors.

Most compiler programs are written to assign a *line number* to each line printed as the result of reading a program except when that printed line is the continuation of the previous line. When several statements are packed on a single card, a line number is assigned to each statement although the line number is not printed. For example, if three statements are packed on line 7, the next line will be line number 10. The line number appears on the extreme left of the output sheet and does not use the print positions available for output. It should never be confused with statement numbers. In Fig. 9-1, line number 8 is the line on which statement number 7 appears. The line number is a convenient method for the compiler program to point out on what line an error occurs. Note the last two error messages in Fig. 9-1.

Errors discovered during the reading or interpretation of the program by the compiler are called *compilation errors.* They are the result of mistakes in punching, using the wrong punctuation in a statement, or forgetting to specify a statement number or define the value for some variable used in an expression. Figure 9-1 shows some compilation errors. The first offense is a warning and says that there is no statement number for the FORMAT statement. The second error shows that on line 4 there is both a * and / next to each other. The third error shows that on line 5 there are unmatched parentheses (around the divisor). The fourth error shows that the WRITE statement was started in column 6 of the card (instead of column 7 as required). When the computer disregards the W in column 6, the rest of the statement does not correspond to any acceptable FORTRAN statement. The fifth error is a reminder that the FORMAT statement, called by the READ statement, had no statement number. The last error notes that statement number 1 was referred to in line 7 (IF statement) and that there is no statement number 1 identified in the program.

These are not all the possible compilation errors, but they do show how the compiler program used for these examples prints out error and warning messages. The difference between an error and a warning is that any error causes the computer to reject the program, while a warning, with no other errors, means that the computer will attempt to execute the program. The warning informs the programmer that the results may be erroneous.

9-3
EXECUTION ERRORS
When an errorless program is read into the computer, an attempt will be made

```
1           DIMENSION Y(10)
2           X=100.
3           Z=1.
4           DO 1 I=1,15
5           X=(X+Z)/100.
6           Y(I)=X
7         1 CONTINUE
8           STOP
9           END


***ERROR***  SUBSCRIPT NUMBER 1 OF Y      HAS THE VALUE        11
        PROGRAM WAS EXECUTING LINE      6 IN ROUTINE M/PROG WHEN TERMINATION
                                                              OCCURRED
```

FIG. 9-2
Execution error.

```
1         DATA ICR,IPR/1,3/
2         X=100.
3         Z=10.
4       1 X=X-Z
5         Y=SQRT(X)
6         WRITE(IPR,100)Y
7         GO TO 1
8     100 FORMAT(1X,F10.4)
**WARNING**  MISSING END STATEMENT;END STATEMENT GENERATED


    9.4868
    8.9443
    8.3666
    7.7460
    7.0711
    6.3246
    5.4772
    4.4721
    3.1623
    0.0000
***ERROR***  X .LT. O. FOR SQRT OR DSQRT OF X

        PROGRAM WAS EXECUTING LINE      5 IN ROUTINE M/PROG WHEN TERMINATION OCCURRED
```

FIG. 9-3
Another execution error.

to execute the statements in the order that the statements are listed. However, there may be some recognizable errors during the execution. Such errors are called *execution errors* and are the result of the programmer asking the computer to execute an impossible instruction, such as: taking the square root of a negative number, dividing by zero, exceeding the storage capacity with a value too large or too small for the system to handle, attempting to print an integer value with a real-mode specification, improperly punched data cards, or a DIMENSION statement not large enough for the array.

Figures 9-2 and 9-3 show two examples of execution errors. In Fig. 9-2 the program contained no compilation errors and so execution started and an error was found. The error message says that subscript number 1 of Y has a value larger than that specified by the DIMENSION statement. (The subscript number refers to the number of the subscript; i.e., a one-dimensional variable has only subscript number 1 while a two-dimensional variable has both subscripts number 1 and number 2.) In such a simple program it is easy to spot the error as caused by the fact that I can vary from 1 to 15 and correct it by changing either the upper limit of the DO statement or the size in the DIMENSION statement. The student should be able to spot another mistake in this program, one that will not show up either during compilation or in execution: What happens after the values are computed? There is no WRITE statement; and so even if the program were run to completion without error, there would be no printout of results. The computer run would have been a complete waste of time and money.

Figure 9-3 shows a program that was accepted with a warning message. The programmer was careless and forgot both STOP and END statements. The computer took care of this by creating its own STOP and END statements and since it was only a warning, allowed the program to start executing. However, the execution ended on an error. The computer was asked to compute the square root of a negative value (less than $\emptyset$). It was fortunate that the program terminated on an error because there is another error in the program. What terminates the program? What if line 4 were 1 X=X+Z? As long as values of X are positive numbers, the program will continue indefinitely. Most computer centers anticipate such human blunders and provide for aborting a program when execution exceeds a fixed time and/or the number of pages specified on a JCL card.

9-4
LOGIC ERRORS

Sometimes a program compiles and executes without error, and yet when looking at the output, the programmer may wonder in amazement at the numbers printed as results. The results are worthless insofar as the intent of the program is concerned. This type of error is often a *logic error* and can be corrected only by carefully studying the flow diagram and program. Sometimes it is necessary to step trial data with known results through the program, statement by statement, before the error is found. In more complex programs than those presented here, correcting logic errors may be exceedingly difficult. A thorough knowledge of all of the ramifications of the problem, its solution, and the nature and magnitude of the anticipated results is required. Time spent in preparing a flow diagram before writing the program is time well spent in preventing this type of error.

MAKING YOUR OWN SUBPROGRAMS 10.

10-1
INTRODUCTION

As stated previously, the principal reason for using the computer is to save time in making long or complex calculations. However, as the student now has discovered, it takes time and thought to prepare a computer program. Many programmers find that as they prepare more and more programs they are using certain calculations or groups of calculations repeatedly. The question could then be asked: Why do the same job over and over? Such repetitive work is, indeed, unnecessary. FORTRAN allows the programmer to prepare groups of instructions called *subprograms* that can be called for and used whenever the main program requires them.

Chapter 6 discussed the library functions available in FORTRAN and how to use them. This chapter will deal with the preparation and use of subprograms that are unique to a particular programmer's needs. Three types of subprograms will be considered: the arithmetic statement function, FUNCTION subprogram, and SUBROUTINE subprogram.

10-2
ARITHMETIC STATEMENT FUNCTION

When a given calculation is used repeatedly within a program, it can be defined as a *function.* When that particular calculation is required, it can be accomplished simply by naming the function. Such a statement is known as an *arithmetic statement function.* It is not really a subprogram because it is a part of the main program; however, for simple calculations, it serves the same purpose.

The general form of the arithmetic statement function is

NAME(A,B,C)=arithmetic expression

where **NAME** is the name of the function, and A, B, and C *are dummy arguments* representing values used in the calculations. The arithmetic expression performs the desired calculation. The rules for forming the function's name are the same as those which apply in forming the name of any variable. The value of a function can be integer or real, and the first letter of the name designates the mode of the result.

The dummy arguments, listed with the name of the function, identify the variables that are used in the calculations. The same variables must be used in the arithmetic expression which establishes the mathematical relationship of the variables. However, when the function is subsequently used (or called) in the program, the *actual* (rather than dummy) arguments (variable names) are listed. The only restrictions are that the actual arguments used in the calling statement must agree in number, mode, and relative position with those used in the defining statement because the actual arguments are substituted, on a one-for-one basis, for the dummy arguments in the defining statement. The defining statement, since it is nonexecutable, must be placed in the program prior to the first executable statement.

As a simple example, suppose that the value of the tangent of an angle must be calculated repeatedly in a given program. An arithmetic statement function defining the tangent could be writen

TAN(A)=SIN(A)/COS(A)

This statment uses two subprograms that are provided as library functions in FORTRAN to define a function that is not available. A later statement calling the tangent function might be

X=Y+2.*TAN(Y)

In determining the value of the function TAN(Y), the computer will compare it with the defining statement and use the actual variable Y in the same way that the dummy variable A was used.

How is the computer programmed to recognize a function? When TAN(Y) is encountered, a check will be made to see if it is specified as a subscripted variable in a DIMENSION statement. Finding that it is not a subscripted variable, a check will be made to see if it is a library function. Finding that it is not a library function, a check will be made to see if there is a defining arithmetic statement function or subprogram where TAN is the name of the function and which has one dummy argument. If there is, execution proceeds; if there is not, an error message is printed and the program is aborted.

For another example, suppose that the roots of a quadratic equation are required frequently in a program. Arithmetic statement functions defining the two roots are

ROOT1(A,B,C)=(−B+SQRT(B**2−4.*A*C))/(2.*A)
ROOT2(A,B,C)=(−B−SQRT(B**2−4.*A*C))/(2.*A)

With these functions so defined, both of the following arithmetic statements are then permissible:

VAL=A*ROOT1(T,(S−R),1.34)
POWER=ROOT2(U,DELTA(1),DELTA(K))**4.5

The value assigned to VAL will be the value of A multiplied by the value of the larger root. The value of ROOT1 is calculated by substituting T for A, (S−R) for B, and 1.34 for C in the defining statement. The value assigned to POWER will be the value of the smaller root raised to the 4.5 power. The value of ROOT2 is calculated by substituting U for A, DELTA(1) for B, and DELTA(K) for C. The value of K must be defined previously in the program.

The arguments (variables) listed in the defining statement are called *dummy arguments* because usually they have no value at that point in the program and the actual use of the function will substitute for these arguments other variables whose values have been defined. These two rules apply to arithmetic statement functions:

1 Dummy arguments must be nonsubscripted variable names, either real or integer. They cannot be constants, other functions, or arithmetic expressions.

2 The actual arguments in the calling statement must agree with the dummy arguments in number, order, and mode. The actual arguments may be variables, constants, other functions, or arithmetic expressions.

The rules and use of the arithmetic statement function are illustrated in Fig. 10-1.

10-3
SUBPROGRAMS

A *subprogram* is added on to the main program following the END statement of the main program. During the time that a main program is being compiled, the computer will look for a subprogram if one is called for by the main program. If a subprogram is present, the computer will compile it and all is well. If no subprogram is found, the main program will be rejected and an error message printed.

A subprogram is a complete program in itself, consisting of a name statement and a list of other FORTRAN statements. The last statement of the subprogram must be an END statement, indicating that the end of the subprogram has been reached. The deck of statement cards used in a sub-program can be used with many different main programs, which is the principal advantage of a subprogram. Once the subprogram has been prepared, the deck of statement cards can be saved and added to any other main program as desired.

The subprogram must communicate with the main program, and it must be

---

The Arithmetic Statement Function

A single arithmetic statement within the main program.

Defines the relationship of a set of variables.

Defining statement must appear before the first executable statement in main program.

General form:

NAME(A, B, C)=arithmetic expression

Example of the defining statement in both mathematical and FORTRAN notation:

$$f(x,y,z) = x^3 + x^2y + xy^2z + y^3z^2 + z^3$$

VALUE(X,Y,Z)=X**3 + X**2*Y + X*Y**2*Z + Y**3*Z**2 + Z**3

Called by using in an arithmetic statement:

ALPHA=VALUE(23.2,15.6,35.2)

or

ALPHA=VALUE(A, B, C)   (If A, B, and C have been previously defined.)

Variables in argument must agree in number, mode, and relative position with defining statement.

FIG. 10-1
Arithmetic statement function.

able to return values to the main program. A subprogram can call on other subprograms, except that a subprogram cannot call itself and two subprograms cannot call each other. There are two types of subprograms with different uses: the FUNCTION subprogram and the SUBROUTINE subprogram. The uses and preparation of each type and how they return values to the main program are the subjects of the next several sections.

10-4
THE RETURN STATEMENT
A subprogram is called for by some action of the main program. In the case of the arithmetic statement function, the function is called by using that function within the program. After the function is evaluated, control automatically returns to the calling statement and calculations continue. When a subprogram is called for, control is not automatically returned to the main program. A RETURN statement, consisting of the single word RETURN, must be used. When a RETURN statement is used in a subprogram, control is returned to the main program in a manner unique to each type of subprogram. Examples of the RETURN statement will be discussed as it is used in each type of subprogram.

10-5

THE FUNCTION SUBPROGRAM

A FUNCTION subprogram is similar to the arithmetic statement function in that it normally calculates and returns only a single value to the main program. It differs from the arithmetic statement function in that a FUNCTION subprogram can consist of as many statements as are required to evaluate a given function. The first statement in a FUNCTION subprogram must be the statement naming the program. The general form is

FUNCTION NAME(A,B,C)

The word FUNCTION identifies the type of subprogram; NAME is the name of the FUNCTION; and A, B, and C are its dummy arguments. The rules for forming the name are the same as those for any FORTRAN variable, with the first letter of the name committing the FUNCTION subprogram to real or integer mode. The dummy arguments, as with the arithmetic statement function, must be nonsubscripted variables or array names. If an array name is used, the subprogram must repeat the DIMENSION statement for the array as it exists in the main program. Then the required FORTRAN statements of the subprogram with RETURN statements must follow where applicable. The FUNCTION's name must appear at least once on the left side of the replacement operator (=). The last statement of the FUNCTION subprogram must be an END statement.

The only values supplied to the subprogram from the main program are the values of the actual variables that are substituted for the dummy arguments of the FUNCTION's name. Any other values for variables used within the subprogram must be defined within the subprogram. The only value returned to the main program from the subprogram is the value assigned to the FUNCTION's name.

As a basic example of a FUNCTION subprogram, suppose that it is desired that the value of a variable VAL depends on the value of some other variable DISP. When DISP is negative, VAL is DISP squared; when DISP is zero, VAL is equal to zero; and when DISP is positive, VAL is the square root of DISP. The FUNCTION subprogram is illustrated in Fig. 10-2, which shows that at any point where the value assigned to the FUNCTION's name is known, control can be returned to the main program. In the case of a FUNCTION subprogram, control is returned to the point in the main program where the subprogram was called.

If the main program were executing the statement Y=3.*VAL(DISP)*S, the subprogram would be called when execution of the statement reached VAL(DISP). The computer identifies VAL(DISP) as a function since VAL is not defined in a DIMENSION statement as a subscripted variable nor is it a library function. The program will then be examined for either an arithmetic statement function or a FUNCTION subprogram with that name. The subprogram will substitute the value of DISP for the dummy argument A and determine the appropriate value of VAL. When that value is determined,

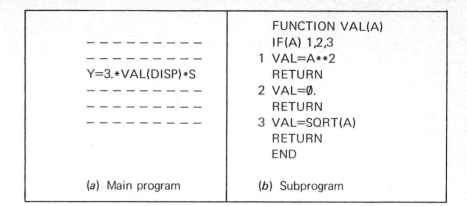

```
                              FUNCTION VAL(A)
  — — — — — — — —             IF(A) 1,2,3
  — — — — — — — —           1 VAL=A**2
  Y=3.*VAL(DISP)*S            RETURN
  — — — — — — — —           2 VAL=Ø.
  — — — — — — — —             RETURN
  — — — — — — — —           3 VAL=SQRT(A)
                              RETURN
                              END

  (a) Main program           (b) Subprogram
```

FIG. 10-2
FUNCTION subprogram.

The FUNCTION Subprogram

Groups of FORTRAN statements referred to by a single name.

A short program compiled independently of the main program.

Information is exchanged between the main program and FUNCTION subprogram, but only one value is returned to the main program.

FUNCTION subprograms are placed separately following END statement of the main program.

May be called by referring to it by name   AREA=ALPHA(A, B) in a single arithmetic statement.

FUNCTION ALPHA(A, B)	Defining statement is the first statement of FUNCTION subprogram.
ALPHA = Expression	Value must be assigned at some point in FUNCTION subprogram.
	First letter of the name (ALPHA) commits FUNCTION subprogram as real or integer mode.
RETURN END	Terminates FUNCTION subprogram; control returns to main program.

FIG. 10-3
Rules for the FUNCTION subprogram.

control will be returned to the main program at the same point where the subprogram was called: VAL(DISP). Now, knowing the value of VAL(DISP), execution of the statement can continue. A brief summation of the rules governing the use of the FUNCTION subprogram is illustrated in Fig. 10-3.

10-6
THE SUBROUTINE SUBPROGRAM
A SUBROUTINE subprogram, though similar to a FUNCTION subprogram,

has four basic differences:

1 A SUBROUTINE subprogram has no value associated with its name. It can return the value of any number of variables back to the main program and receive the value of any number of variables from the main program provided that these variables are matched with the dummy arguments listed after the name of the SUBROUTINE.

2 Since the name of a SUBROUTINE subprogram has no value, there is no mode (integer or real) associated with the first letter of the name. The name may consist of a maximum of any six letters or numbers provided that the first character is a letter.

3 Since the name of a SUBROUTINE subprogram has no value, it cannot be called simply by using its name in the main program. Instead, a CALL statement is required in the main program to start the operation of the SUBROUTINE.

4 Because of the preceding requirement, when control is returned to the main program, it returns to the statement immediately following the CALL statement.

The **CALL** statement in general form is

CALL NAME(X,Y,Z)

where **NAME** is the name of the **SUBROUTINE** and X, Y, and Z are the actual arguments (variables) whose values are to be used in the subprogram.
    The first statement in the subprogram must be one whose general form is

SUBROUTINE NAME(A,B,C)

where **SUBROUTINE** identifies the type of subprogram, **NAME** is the name of the **SUBROUTINE**, and A, B, and C are dummy arguments whose values are to be used within the subprogram. If any of the arguments is a subscripted variable, the name of the dummy argument is not written in subscripted form. In this case, the next statement must be a **DIMENSION** statement repeating the size of the array as defined in the main program. The statements of the subprogram then follow. The **SUBROUTINE** subprogram is terminated by the two statements **RETURN** and **END** in that order. A brief summation of the rules governing the use of the **SUBROUTINE** subprogram is illustrated in Fig. 10-4.
    As an example of the use of a **SUBROUTINE** subprogram, the grade problem presented previously in Sec. 8-7 will be revised. The largest part of that problem was sorting and rearranging the data. Yet sorting data is applicable to many different situations. Since no such library function is available, a subprogram will be written and applied to the grade problem. The logic of the left-hand portion of the flow diagram shown in Fig. 8-6 can be used with

FIG. 10-4
Rules for the SUBROUTINE
subprogram.

The SUBROUTINE Subprogram	
A short program compiled independently of the main program and referred to by a single name.	
Can return more than one value to the main program.	
SUBROUTINE subprograms are placed separately following the END statement of the main program.	
SUBROUTINE subprograms are called by a CALL statement before SUBROUTINE name.	CALL ALPHA(A, B, C)
SUBROUTINE ALPHA(A, B, C)	Defining statement is first statement of SUBROUTINE subprogram.
	First letter of name *does not* commit mode.
RETURN	Terminates SUBROUTINE subprogram; control returns to main program.
END	

slight modifications for the SUBROUTINE subprogram. Name the subprogram SORTI and use arguments I, J, and K, where I represents the array of original data, J represents the array of data arranged in descending order, and K represents the number of data to be sorted. To make the subprogram more general, set the maximum size of the two arrays at K since K will be the amount of data. This obviously is a sorter for integer numbers; a sorter for real numbers could also be made by a similar program with the variable names changed. The completed subprogram is shown in Fig. 10-5, lines 29 to 42.

The main program has been slightly revised (Fig. 10-5, lines 1 to 28) to make possible the reading of any number of grades up to and including 1ØØ grades. Note that if more than 1ØØ data cards are used, the IF statement on line 8 stops the reading of cards, thus preventing an execution error due to exceeding the maximum number of subscripted values defined in the DIMENSION statement.

The results of this program are shown in Fig. 10-6. Since the same data are used in this problem as in the problem as presented in Sec. 8-7, the results of Figs. 8-8 and 10-6 are identical.

PROBLEMS
10-1
Often, in scientific work, the area under a curve must be computed. One method for accomplishing this computation is Simpson's rule. Figure 10-7 illustrates Simpson's rule, where the area under the curve between the limits *a*

```
 1            DATA ICR,IPR/1,3/
 2            DIMENSION IGRADE(100),JGRADE(100)
 3            I=1
 4          1 READ(ICR,100)IGRADE(I),LCAR
 5        100 FORMAT(2I3)
 6            IF(LCAR.GT.0)GO TO 3
 7            I=I+1
 8            IF(I.GT.100)GO TO 2
 9            GO TO 1
10          2 I=I-1
11            WRITE(IPR,150)
12        150 FORMAT(1X,'READING HALTED BECAUSE 100 CARDS HAVE BEEN READ.',///)
13          3 CALL SORTI(IGRADE,JGRADE,I)
14            ITOT=0
15            DO 4 INDEX=1,I
16          4 ITOT=ITOT+JGRADE(INDEX)
17            TOT=ITOT
18            X=I
19            AVE=TOT/X
20            WRITE(IPR,200)
21        200 FORMAT(4X,'ORDER OF GRADES',/)
22            DO 5 LIST=1,I
23          5 WRITE(IPR,300)JGRADE(LIST)
24        300 FORMAT(10X,I3)
25            WRITE(IPR,400)AVE
26        400 FORMAT(1X,'THE AVERAGE GRADE =',F6.2)
27            STOP
28            END

29            SUBROUTINE SORTI(I,J,K)
30            DIMENSION I(K),J(K)
31            DO 2 L=1,K
32            IBIG=I(1)
33            N=1
34            DO 1 M=2,K
35            IF(IBIG.GT.I(M))GO TO 1
36            IBIG=I(M)
37            N=M
38          1 CONTINUE
39            I(N)=0
40          2 J(L)=IBIG
41            RETURN
42            END
```

FIG. 10-5
Grade problem using a sorting
SUBROUTINE.

```
ORDER OF GRADES

          100
          100
           99
           98
           93
           91
           90
           89
           88
           87
           86
           85
           85
           79
           78
           76
           75
           74
           73
           72
           72
           70
           65
           63
           54
THE AVERAGE GRADE = 81.68
```

FIG. 10-6
Printout of the grade problem
shown in Fig. 10-5. (Compare
with that shown in Fig. 8-8.)

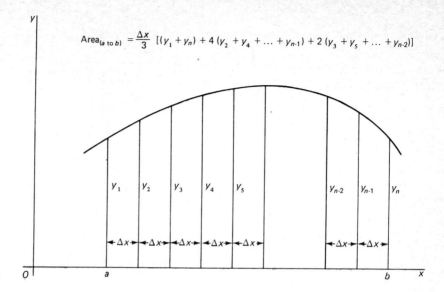

FIG. 10-7
Simpson's rule.

and b is to be determined. The area is divided into any number of even intervals. After the value of each ordinate is determined, the value of the area is found by the formula

$$A = \frac{\Delta x}{3} \left[(y_1 + y_n) + 4(y_2 + y_4 + \cdots + y_{n-1}) + 2(y_3 + y_5 + \cdots + y_{n-2}) \right]$$

Note that since the distance between a and b is divided into an even number of intervals, the number of ordinates will always be one more than the number of intervals and, therefore, the value of n in y_n will always be an odd number.

Write a program to compute the area under any curve. Use an arithmetic statement function to define the curve. The next two statements should specify the x value of the minimum and maximum ordinates. Divide the distance between these two ordinates into an even number of intervals such that the maximum value of the interval is less than 0.02. The remaining portion of the main program should calculate the values of all the resulting ordinates and print the value of the area. Use a FUNCTION subprogram to calculate the area. Then determine the area under a sine curve between $y = 0$ and $y = \pi$. Note that by changing only three statements—the arithmetic statement function and the two statements specifying values of the minimum and maximum ordinates—the program can be used to determine the area under any curve. Students who have studied calculus will recognize this as a computerized approximation of integration.

10-2
Revise Prob. 8-3 so that the minimum as well as maximum value of the matrix is found by using a SUBROUTINE subprogram.

10-3

An artillery gun position and potential targets are located by rectangular coordinates. A table of powder charges to be used for various ranges is given, as are the minimum and maximum azimuths defining the safety limits for firing the gun at that position. The maximum range of the gun is also given. Gun and target coordinates are given as eight-digit integer numbers where the first four digits are the *X* coordinates to the nearest 10 m and the second four digits are the *Y* coordinates to the nearest 10 m. Azimuth is defined as a clockwise angle measured from the north and can vary from 0 to 360°.

Write a program to determine the range in meters and azimuth in degrees from the gun position to the target and the appropriate charge to use. Check the azimuth against the safety limits and the range against the maximum range. Use a SUBROUTINE subprogram to calculate the range and azimuth, and use a FUNCTION subprogram to determine the charge.

The coordinates of the gun position are 30005000. The minimum safe azimuth is 42°, and the maximum safe azimuth is 235°. The maximum range is 15,000 m. The table of ranges and charges is

Range, m	Charge
0–3000	1
3001–6000	2
6001–9000	3
9001–12,000	4
Over 12,000	5

The possible targets are at coordinates 37415310, 32255000, 33834032, 38733925, 30004525, 34505515, 25354715, 38633675, and 30005000.

Be careful when calculating azimuths since in some cases the determination of the size of the angle may result in dividing by zero. If this occurs, an execution error will halt the program. Since the coordinates are given only to the nearest 10 m, the range calculations cannot have a greater precision. However, the printout of the range should show the range in meters.

HOW ACCURATE 11.
IS THE
COMPUTER?

11-1
INTRODUCTION

With the first discovery that the computer is not the unfailingly accurate calculator of all values to any precision, the new programmer loses an illusion common to most people unfamiliar with computer operations. After recovering from this initial shock, the programmer settles down into the real world of computers with a better appreciation of their actual capabilities and limitations. This chapter will discuss some of these limitations and what can be done about them.

11-2
INCREMENTAL INACCURACIES

Section 1-4 stated that only values that were exact powers of 2 could be precisely stored by the computer, which includes all whole numbers and such fractional numbers as $\frac{1}{2}$ (Ø.5), $\frac{1}{4}$ (Ø.25), and $\frac{1}{8}$ (Ø.125). At that point an illustrative program to demonstrate this fact was not considered advisable because the output statements had not yet been discussed and more questions would have been raised than settled. However, now we can write and run such a program.

Figure 11-1 shows what happens when a number is incremented by a value such as Ø.Ø1, which is not an exact power of 2. Theoretically each value should be Ø.Ø1 larger than its previous value. When the two-hundredth value of VAR is calculated, the expected value should be 2.99. But, due to accumulated inaccuracies of the approximate value of Ø.Ø1 that were stored in the computer, it is not. The program shows 200 successive values; note how the error gradually increases. To test to see if the two-hundredth value has

```
     1           DATA ICR,IPR/1,3/
     2           DIMENSION VAR(200)
     3           VAR(1)=1.0
     4           DELTA=0.01
     5           DO 1 I=2,200
     6         1 VAR(I)=VAR(I-1)+DELTA
     7           WRITE(IPR,100)(VAR(I),I=1,200)
     8       100 FORMAT(1X,10F10.6)
     9           STOP
    10           END
```

1.000000	1.009999	1.019999	1.029998	1.039997	1.049996	1.059996	1.069995	1.079994	1.089993
1.099993	1.109992	1.119991	1.129991	1.139990	1.149989	1.159988	1.169988	1.179987	1.189986
1.199986	1.209985	1.219984	1.229983	1.239983	1.249982	1.259981	1.269980	1.279980	1.289979
1.299978	1.309978	1.319977	1.329976	1.339975	1.349975	1.359974	1.369973	1.379972	1.389972
1.399971	1.409970	1.419970	1.429969	1.439968	1.449967	1.459967	1.469966	1.479965	1.489964
1.499964	1.509963	1.519962	1.529962	1.539961	1.549960	1.559959	1.569959	1.579958	1.589957
1.599957	1.609956	1.619955	1.629954	1.639954	1.649953	1.659952	1.669951	1.679951	1.689950
1.699949	1.709949	1.719948	1.729947	1.739946	1.749946	1.759945	1.769944	1.779943	1.789943
1.799942	1.809941	1.819941	1.829940	1.839939	1.849938	1.859938	1.869937	1.879936	1.889935
1.899935	1.909934	1.919933	1.929933	1.939932	1.949931	1.959930	1.969930	1.979929	1.989928
1.999928	2.009927	2.019926	2.029925	2.039925	2.049924	2.059923	2.069922	2.079922	2.089921
2.099920	2.109920	2.119919	2.129918	2.139917	2.149917	2.159916	2.169915	2.179914	2.189914
2.199913	2.209912	2.219912	2.229911	2.239910	2.249909	2.259909	2.269908	2.279907	2.289907
2.299906	2.309905	2.319904	2.329904	2.339903	2.349902	2.359901	2.369901	2.379900	2.389899
2.399899	2.409898	2.419897	2.429896	2.439896	2.449895	2.459894	2.469893	2.479893	2.489892
2.499891	2.509891	2.519890	2.529889	2.539888	2.549888	2.559887	2.569886	2.579885	2.589885
2.599884	2.609883	2.619883	2.629882	2.639881	2.649880	2.659880	2.669879	2.679878	2.689878
2.699877	2.709876	2.719875	2.729875	2.739874	2.749873	2.759872	2.769872	2.779871	2.789870
2.799870	2.809869	2.819868	2.829867	2.839867	2.849866	2.859865	2.869864	2.879864	2.889863
2.899862	2.909862	2.919861	2.929860	2.939859	2.949859	2.959858	2.969857	2.979856	2.989856

FIG. 11-1
Precision loss due to incrementing value.

```
     1           DATA ICR,IPR/1,3/
     2           DIMENSION VAR(200)
     3           X=100.
     4           D=1.
     5           VAR(1)=1.
     6           DO 1 I=2,200
     7           X=X+D
     8         1 VAR(I)=X/100.
     9           WRITE(IPR,100)(VAR(J),J=1,200)
    10       100 FORMAT(1X,10F10.6)
    11           STOP
    12           END
```

1.000000	1.009999	1.020000	1.030000	1.040000	1.049999	1.059999	1.070000	1.080000	1.089999
1.099999	1.110000	1.120000	1.129999	1.139999	1.150000	1.160000	1.169999	1.179999	1.190000
1.200000	1.209999	1.219999	1.230000	1.240000	1.250000	1.259999	1.270000	1.280000	1.290000
1.299999	1.309999	1.320000	1.330000	1.339999	1.349999	1.360000	1.370000	1.379999	1.389999
1.400000	1.410000	1.419999	1.429999	1.440000	1.450000	1.459999	1.469999	1.480000	1.490000
1.500000	1.509999	1.520000	1.530000	1.540000	1.549999	1.559999	1.570000	1.580000	1.589999
1.599999	1.610000	1.620000	1.629999	1.639999	1.650000	1.660000	1.669999	1.679999	1.690000
1.700000	1.709999	1.719999	1.730000	1.740000	1.750000	1.759999	1.770000	1.780000	1.790000
1.799999	1.809999	1.820000	1.830000	1.839999	1.849999	1.860000	1.870000	1.879999	1.889999
1.900000	1.910000	1.919999	1.929999	1.940000	1.950000	1.959999	1.969999	1.980000	1.990000
2.000000	2.009999	2.020000	2.030000	2.040000	2.049999	2.059999	2.070000	2.080000	2.089999
2.099999	2.110000	2.120000	2.129999	2.139999	2.150000	2.160000	2.169999	2.179999	2.190000
2.200000	2.209999	2.219999	2.230000	2.240000	2.250000	2.259999	2.270000	2.280000	2.290000
2.299999	2.309999	2.320000	2.330000	2.339999	2.349999	2.360000	2.370000	2.379999	2.389999
2.400000	2.410000	2.419999	2.429999	2.440000	2.450000	2.459999	2.469999	2.480000	2.490000
2.500000	2.509999	2.520000	2.530000	2.540000	2.549999	2.559999	2.570000	2.580000	2.589999
2.599999	2.610000	2.620000	2.629999	2.639999	2.650000	2.660000	2.669999	2.679999	2.690000
2.700000	2.709999	2.719999	2.730000	2.740000	2.750000	2.759999	2.770000	2.780000	2.790000
2.799999	2.809999	2.820000	2.830000	2.839999	2.849999	2.860000	2.870000	2.879999	2.889999
2.900000	2.910000	2.919999	2.929999	2.940000	2.950000	2.959999	2.969999	2.980000	2.990000

FIG. 11-2
Incrementing to avoid accumulative errors.

```
 1              DATA ICR,IPR/1,3/
 2              DIMENSION VAR(200)
 3              X=100.
 4              D=1.
 5              VAR(1)=1.
 6              DO 1 I=2,200
 7              X=X+D
 8            1 VAR(I)=X/100.
 9              WRITE(IPR,100)(VAR(K),K=1,200)
10          100 FORMAT(1X,10F10.4)
11              STOP
12              END
```

1.0000	1.0100	1.0200	1.0300	1.0400	1.0500	1.0600	1.0700	1.0800	1.0900
1.1000	1.1100	1.1200	1.1300	1.1400	1.1500	1.1600	1.1700	1.1800	1.1900
1.2000	1.2100	1.2200	1.2300	1.2400	1.2500	1.2600	1.2700	1.2800	1.2900
1.3000	1.3100	1.3200	1.3300	1.3400	1.3500	1.3600	1.3700	1.3800	1.3900
1.4000	1.4100	1.4200	1.4300	1.4400	1.4500	1.4600	1.4700	1.4800	1.4900
1.5000	1.5100	1.5200	1.5300	1.5400	1.5500	1.5600	1.5700	1.5800	1.5900
1.6000	1.6100	1.6200	1.6300	1.6400	1.6500	1.6600	1.6700	1.6800	1.6900
1.7000	1.7100	1.7200	1.7300	1.7400	1.7500	1.7600	1.7700	1.7800	1.7900
1.8000	1.8100	1.8200	1.8300	1.8400	1.8500	1.8600	1.8700	1.8800	1.8900
1.9000	1.9100	1.9200	1.9300	1.9400	1.9500	1.9600	1.9700	1.9800	1.9900
2.0000	2.0100	2.0200	2.0300	2.0400	2.0500	2.0600	2.0700	2.0800	2.0900
2.1000	2.1100	2.1200	2.1300	2.1400	2.1500	2.1600	2.1700	2.1800	2.1900
2.2000	2.2100	2.2200	2.2300	2.2400	2.2500	2.2600	2.2700	2.2800	2.2900
2.3000	2.3100	2.3200	2.3300	2.3400	2.3500	2.3600	2.3700	2.3800	2.3900
2.4000	2.4100	2.4200	2.4300	2.4400	2.4500	2.4600	2.4700	2.4800	2.4900
2.5000	2.5100	2.5200	2.5300	2.5400	2.5500	2.5600	2.5700	2.5800	2.5900
2.6000	2.6100	2.6200	2.6300	2.6400	2.6500	2.6600	2.6700	2.6800	2.6900
2.7000	2.7100	2.7200	2.7300	2.7400	2.7500	2.7600	2.7700	2.7800	2.7900
2.8000	2.8100	2.8200	2.8300	2.8400	2.8500	2.8600	2.8700	2.8800	2.8900
2.9000	2.9100	2.9200	2.9300	2.9400	2.9500	2.9600	2.9700	2.9800	2.9900

FIG. 11-3
Effect of a narrow field width
on apparent accuracy.

been reached, knowing that the value should be 2.99, the following IF statement might be written:

IF(VAR.EQ.2.99) GO TO 6

But the program will never branch to statement number 6 because the variable VAR will never exactly equal 2.99. With the understanding that the value 2.99 might never be exactly reached, how can a branch after the two-hundredth value be programmed?

A decision must be made on some acceptable range of accuracy. This error may be plus or minus, depending upon the computer. Also, since the amount of error depends on the word size of the computer, no hard and fast rules can be given as to the amount of error. The programmer must learn from experience what to expect from a particular computer. In our present example, the following logical IF statement might be used:

IF (VAR.GT.2.989.AND.VAR.LT.2.991) GO TO 6

This statement is written to bracket the expected value and allows no other incremented value to satisfy it. The statement will cause the computer to branch to statement number 6 after the two-hundredth value.

If this inaccuracy is not acceptable, there is a way to circumvent it using a few more FORTRAN statements. The procedure is to multiply the value to be incremented and the value of the increment by a multiplier which will make the increment a whole number. Then, after the new value has been incremented by the new increment, dividing by the multiplier will give the desired value. Figure 11-2 shows the program and the results of 199 increments (200 successive values) of the same number used in Fig. 11-1. Note that inaccuracies do appear, but they are not additive and soon disappear. However, if a test is required to determine if a particular value has been reached, the .AND. relationship of the preceding IF statement must be used.

Figure 11-3 shows the same program given in Fig. 11-2, with one important change: The specification in the FORMAT statement is changed from F10.6 to F10.4. The printed results appear to be accurate and are correct to four decimal places. Apparently the incrementing has been done exactly as was intended. Compare these values with the values shown in Fig. 11-2. The reason for this apparent accuracy is the rounding-off process to print the results with four decimal places.

Seeing the printed results shown in Fig. 11-3 might lead one to assume that the ninetieth value is exactly 1.89 and that one could test for that value. But the value actually in storage is more nearly the value shown in Fig. 11-2 (1.88999), and therefore a test for equality with 1.89 will fail.

If there are only a few increments (30 to 40) to be done, it is normally unnecessary to apply the multiplier method of incrementing.

11-3
CALCULATION INACCURACIES

Usually when the computer's results do not correspond to expected values, the fault lies in a logic error made by the programmer. However, sometimes the discrepancy is due to the limitations of the computer. An example of this condition is illustrated in the following problem.

Assume a flat sheet with dimensions $A \times B$, as shown in Fig. 11-4a. Squares of size X are removed from the four corners of the sheet, and the remaining sides are folded up, forming a box, Fig. 11-4b. What value of X will result in a box with the largest volume? The answer can be determined by applying the calculus or by trial and error, that is, assuming different values for X and looking for the largest volume. This trial-and-error method is used in the flow diagram shown in Fig. 11-5, and the program and printed results are shown in Fig. 11-6. If the volume of the first line of the results is computed by hand, it will be found that when $X=4.17$, the volume (to five decimal places) should be 1157.40685 instead of 1157.40500, the value shown.

The error is not due to incrementing; there are fewer than 20 iterations. Neither is the error one of logic. The error occurs because the "word" size of the computer was exceeded during calculations, resulting in a truncation of values. The error is quite small, only 0.00016 percent. This condition has appeared in previous programs. For example, the value shown in Fig. 4-9 for the area of the circle when the radius is 125 is not accurate to eight significant figures. The computer user must be aware of the possibilities of inaccuracies caused by truncation when results involve six or more significant figures.

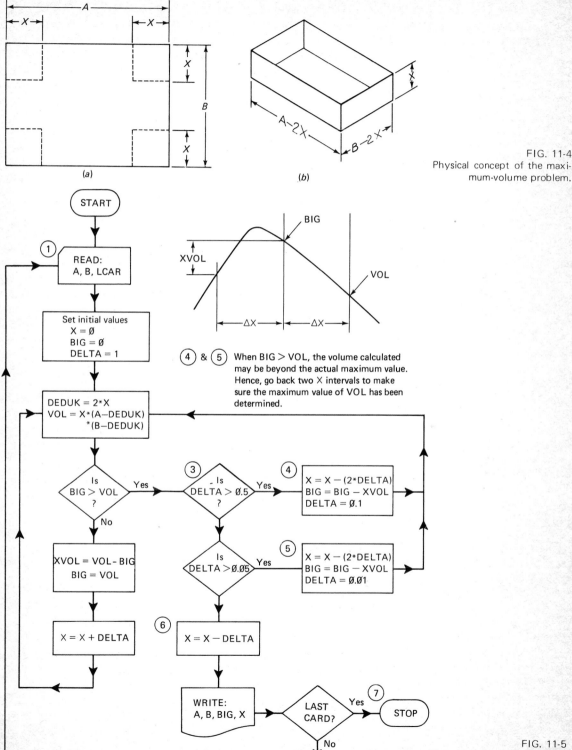

FIG. 11-4
Physical concept of the maximum-volume problem.

When BIG > VOL, the volume calculated may be beyond the actual maximum value. Hence, go back two X intervals to make sure the maximum value of VOL has been determined.

FIG. 11-5
Flow diagram for the maximum-volume problem.

```
 1              DATA ICR,IPR/1,3/
 2            1 READ(ICR,100)A,B,LCAR
 3          100 FORMAT(2F6.2,I3)
 4              X=0.0
 5              BIG=0.0
 6              DELTA=1.0
 7            2 DEDUK=2.0*X
 8              VOL=X*(A-DEDUK)*(B-DEDUK)
 9              IF(BIG.GT.VOL)GO TO 3
10              XVOL=VOL-BIG
11              BIG=VOL
12              X=X+DELTA
13              GO TO 2
14            3 IF(DELTA.GT.0.5)GO TO 4
15              IF(DELTA.GT.0.05)GO TO 5
16              GO TO 6
17            4 X=X-(2.0*DELTA)
18              IBIG=BIG-XVOL
19              BIG=IBIG
20              DELTA=0.1
21              GO TO 2
22            5 X=X-(2.0*DELTA)
23              IBIG=BIG-XVOL
24              BIG=IBIG
25              DELTA=0.01
26              GO TO 2
27            6 X=X-DELTA
28              WRITE(IPR,200)A,B,BIG,X
29          200 FORMAT(1X,'IF A=',F7.2,' AND B=',F7.2,', THE VOLUME=',F12.5,' WHEN
              1 X=',F6.2,/)
30              IF(LCAR)1,1,7
31            7 STOP
32              END
```

```
IF A=  25.00 AND B=  25.00, THE VOLUME=  1157.40500 WHEN X=  4.17

IF A=  25.00 AND B=  50.00, THE VOLUME=  3007.03000 WHEN X=  5.28

IF A=  25.00 AND B=  75.00, THE VOLUME=  4930.69900 WHEN X=  5.64

IF A=  25.00 AND B= 100.00, THE VOLUME=  6870 46400 WHEN X=  5.81

IF A=  50.00 AND B=  50.00, THE VOLUME=  9259.25700 WHEN X=  8.33

IF A=  50.00 AND B=  75.00, THE VOLUME= 16504.77000 WHEN X=  9.81

IF A=  50.00 AND B= 100.00, THE VOLUME= 24056.25C00 WHEN X= 10.57

IF A=  75.00 AND B=  75.00, THE VOLUME= 31250.00000 WHEN X= 12.50

IF A=  75.00 AND B= 100.00, THE VOLUME= 47379.73C00 WHEN X= 14.14

IF A= 100.00 AND B= 100.00, THE VOLUME= 74074.06000 WHEN X= 16.67
```

FIG. 11-6
Maximum-volume problem using single-precision variables.

11-4
DOUBLE PRECISION

If the slight inaccuracies of calculations discussed in Sec. 11-3 are not acceptable, a technique called *double precision* is available in FORTRAN to reduce and sometimes eliminate the inaccuracies. The computer may be programmed to use two "words" to store a given value, thus effectively doubling the number of significant digits which can be handled. The declaration statement to accomplish this is, in general form,

DOUBLE PRECISION A, X, . . . , N

where **DOUBLE PRECISION** tells the computer that each of the variables listed is to be stored in two "words." The variables listed, if there are more than one, are separated by commas. The following rules are applicable in **DOUBLE PRECISION** arithmetic operations:

1 Whenever double precision is to be used, the DOUBLE PRECISION declaration statement must appear in the program before any executable statements.

2 If an expression is mixed, with some variables or constants in double precision and others in single precision, the expression will be evaluated in double precision. Thus the expression 2.0*X will be evaluated in double precision if the variable X has been declared to be a double-precision variable by a DOUBLE PRECISION declaration statement. It is a waste of time to write the constant, in this instance, in double-precision form (see rule 5) since 2.0 is a whole number and therefore represented precisely by the computer. However if the constant were 2.1, greater accuracy would be attained by writing it in double-precision form.

3 If the variable to the left of the replacement operator (=) is declared DOUBLE PRECISION, the value of the associated expression will be stored in double precision.

4 If the variable to the left of the replacement operator is not declared DOUBLE PRECISION, the value of the associated expression (if a variable in it is in double precision) will be calculated in double precision and the result truncated and stored in a single "word."

5 Any constant to be double-precision must be written in exponential form with the letter D used in place of the letter E. Thus 0.3D3 is a double-precision constant while 0.3E3 is stored in a single "word."

6 The functions listed in Chap. 6 are also available in double precision by placing a D in front of the function name, as in DSQRT. The variable or expression used as the argument must be declared previously as double-precision.

7 When using double precision with subscripted variables, the DOUBLE PRECISION declaration statement eliminates the need for a DIMENSION statement. For example, the DIMENSION declaration statement for single-precision subscripted variables is DIMENSION A(10),X(5,5). A DOUBLE PRECISION declaration statement for the same variables would be DOUBLE PRECISION A(10),X(5,5). This statement both declares the variables to be double-precision and specifies the storage space required for the arrays.

The program described in Sec. 11-2 is revised for double-precision calculations and is illustrated in Fig. 11-7; the results are shown in Fig. 11-8. Note that the value of the volume of the 25X25 sheet now includes 10 significant figures and is accurate to 5 decimal places. The use of double precision can increase the accuracy of calculations but at the cost of some increase of computer time. Before deciding to use double precision, the need for increased accuracy should be carefully weighed against the increased cost for additional time.

Note that the first assigned values of the variables X and DELTA are expressed as double-precision constants. This is not necessary. The two state-

```
1              DATA ICR,IPR/1,3/
2              DOUBLE PRECISION X,BIG,DELTA,DEDUK,VOL,XVOL
3          1 READ(ICR,100)A,B,LCAR
4        100 FORMAT(2F6.2,I3)
C SET INITIAL VALUE FOR SIDE OF SQUARE TO BE REMOVED.
5              X=0.0D0
C SET INITIAL VALUE OF VOLUME IN BIG. BIG WILL ALWAYS CONTAIN THE LAST VOLUME.
6              BIG=0.0D0
C SET FIRST VALUE FOR INCREMENTING THE THE SIZE OF THE SQUARE TO BE REMOVED.
7              DELTA=1.0D0
C DETERMINE THE AMOUNT TO BE DEDUCTED FROM THE SIDES OF THE BASIC RECTANGLE.
8          2 DEDUK=2.0*X
C DETERMINE THE VOLUME AFTER FOLDING UP THE SIDES.
9              VOL=X*(A-DEDUK)*(B-DEDUK)
C LOOK FOR A DECREASE IN VOLUME.
10             IF(BIG.GT.VOL)GO TO 3
C DETERMINE THE CHANGE IN VOLUME.
11             XVOL=VOL-BIG
C PUT VOLUME JUST CALCULATED INTO BIG.
12             BIG=VOL
C INCREMENT THE VALUE OF THE SIDE OF THE SQUARE.
13             X=X+DELTA
C REPEAT CALCULATIONS.
14             GO TO 2
C RUN THROUGH AN 'IF' FILTER TO DETERMINE THE VALUE OF THE NEXT INCREMENT TO BE
C USED FOR THE SIDE OF THE SQUARE.
15         3 IF(DELTA.GT.0.5)GO TO 4
16             IF(DELTA.GT.0.05)GO TO 5
17             GO TO 6
C RESET THE VALUE OF THE SIDE OF THE SQUARE BACK TWO INCREMENTS TO INSURE THAT
C IT IS LESS THAN THAT NECESSARY TO PRODUCE THE LARGEST VOLUME.
18         4 X=X-(2.0*DELTA)
C RESET BIG TO CORRESPOND TO THE X JUST SET. BIG MUST BE TRUNCATED TO REMOVE
C ERROR CAUSING RESIDUALS FOR THE NEXT TEST OF (BIG.GT.VOL).
19             IBIG=BIG-XVOL
20             BIG=IBIG
C SET NEXT VALUE OF INCREMENT.
21             DELTA=1.0D-1
C REPEAT CALCULATIONS.
22             GO TO 2
23         5 X=X-(2.0*DELTA)
24             IBIG=BIG-XVOL
25             BIG=IBIG
C SET NEXT VALUE OF INCREMENT.
26             DELTA=1.0D-2
C REPEAT CALCULATIONS.
27             GO TO 2
C THE VOLUME IS NOW CALCULATED TO THE DESIRED ACCURACY. SINCE THE LAST VOLUME
C SHOWED A DECREASE, BIG IS THE MAXIMUM VOLUME AND THEREFORE X MUST BE REDUCED
C BY ONE INCREMENT TO CORRESPOND.
28         6 X=X-DELTA
29             WRITE(IPR,200)A,B,BIG,X
30        200 FORMAT(1X,'IF A=',F7.2,' AND B=',F7.2,', THE VOLUME=',F12.5,' WHEN
         1 X=',F6.2,/)
C CHECK TO SEE IF LAST DATA CARD HAS BEEN READ.
31             IF(LCAR)1,1,7
32         7 STOP
33             END
```

FIG. 11-7
Program for the maximum-volume problem with comment cards using double-precision variables.

ments could just as well have been X=0.0 and DELTA=1.0 since both constants are whole numbers and therefore represented exactly in the computer. Their values are stored in double precision because the variables were declared to be double-precision variables. The reason they were written in double precision was to provide a few more examples of how to express double-precision constants.

Note also the liberal use of comment cards in the program illustrated in Fig. 11-7. Compare the ease of understanding the reason for each FORTRAN statement in Fig. 11-7 with the similar program shown in Fig. 11-6. The program of Fig. 11-7, together with the flow diagram of Fig. 11-5, is an example of a documented program.

```
IF A=   25.00 AND B=   25.00, THE VOLUME=   1157.40685 WHEN X=  4.17
IF A=   25.00 AND B=   50.00, THE VOLUME=   3007.03181 WHEN X=  5.28
IF A=   25.00 AND B=   75.00, THE VOLUME=   4930.70458 WHEN X=  5.64
IF A=   25.00 AND B=  100.00, THE VOLUME=   6870.46676 WHEN X=  5.81
IF A=   50.00 AND B=   50.00, THE VOLUME=   9259.25815 WHEN X=  8.33
IF A=   50.00 AND B=   75.00, THE VOLUME=  16504.77956 WHEN X=  9.81
IF A=   50.00 AND B=  100.00, THE VOLUME=  24056.25877 WHEN X= 10.57
IF A=   75.00 AND B=   75.00, THE VOLUME=  31250.00000 WHEN X= 12.50
IF A=   75.00 AND B=  100.00, THE VOLUME=  47379.72378 WHEN X= 14.14
IF A=  100.00 AND B=  100.00, THE VOLUME=  74074.07185 WHEN X= 16.67
```

FIG. 11-8
Double-precision results for
maximum-volume problem.

11-5
CONCLUSION

The material in this and preceding chapters provides the basic information for programming the solutions to reasonably complex problems. As readers gain experience they will gradually realize the need to know more about the total power of FORTRAN IV. A list of the statements available in most versions of FORTRAN IV is shown in Appendix A, together with a brief explanation of each statement. As the need for these additional statements occurs, it is suggested that experienced programmers and systems manuals be consulted for more detailed information.

APPENDIX A.

FORTRAN IV STATEMENTS AND LIBRARY FUNCTIONS

TABLE A-1 FORTRAN IV STATEMENTS EXPLAINED IN TEXT

Statement	Example	Section No.
arithmetic statement	Y=X*A+B	2-7
CALL EXIT	CALL EXIT	2-11
CALL NAME(X,Y,Z)	CALL SORT(A,B)	10-6
CONTINUE	CONTINUE	4-5
DATA list/$a_1,a_2, \ldots , a_n$/	DATA A,B,I/3.∅,4.5,6/	3-19
DIMENSION list	DIMENSION A(1∅),B(2∅,15)	8-3
DO i $j=l,m,n$	DO 1∅ I=1,11,2	4-4
DOUBLE PRECISION list	DOUBLE PRECISION A,S	11-4
END	END	2-11, 10-5, 10-6
FORMAT(specifications)	FORMAT(3F1∅.5)	3-3, 3-4
		3-5, 3-7, 3-8, 3-9, 3-10
FUNCTION NAME(A,B,C)	FUNCTION VAL(A)	10-5
GO TO n	GO TO 1∅	4-2
IF(V)n_1,n_2,n_3	IF(LCAR)1,1,7	4-3
IF(logic)statement	IF(A.GT.B)X=A*B	7-3
INTEGER list	INTEGER A, DELTA	2-8
NAME(A, B, C)=expression	TAN(A)=SIN(A)/COS(A)	10-2
PRINT, list	PRINT, A,X,J	3-12
READ(i,j)list	READ(1,1∅∅)A,B,C,	3-2
READ, list	READ, A,X,J	3-11
READ(i,j,END=m)list	READ(5,1∅∅,END=1∅)A,B,J	4-8
REAL list	REAL LOAD, MASS	2-8
RETURN	RETURN	10-4
STOP	STOP	2-11
SUBROUTINE NAME(A,B,C)	SUBROUTINE SORT(A,B)	10-6
WRITE(k,l)list	WRITE(3,1∅∅)A,B,C	3-8

123

TABLE A-2 FORTRAN IV STATEMENTS NOT EXPLAINED IN TEXT

Statement	Example	Explanation
ASSIGN m TO K	ASSIGN 5 TO K	Assigns value of statement number K; used with assigned GO TO to set K.
BACKSPACE n	BACKSPACE 6	Tape 6 is to move back one record. A record can be any number of characters.
COMMON list	COMMON A,B(14)	When used in both main and subprogram, it places data from both in same storage locations. Arrays may be dimensioned without using DIMENSION statement.
COMPLEX list	COMPLEX A,X	Variables listed are complex variables.
END FILE n	END FILE 6	Causes tape mark showing end of record to be put on tape 6.
EQUIVALENCE(list)	EQUIVALENCE(LC, LCR),(X(1),Y(3))	Usually used to conserve storage space by storing more than one variable in the same space. It can also be used to correct different spellings for the same variable.
EXTERNAL list	EXTERNAL SORT, COS	If an argument in a statement calling a function or subroutine is itself a subprogram, it must be listed in this statement.
GO TO$(n_1,n_2, \ldots , n_m)$,i	GO TO(7,1∅)K	Computed GO TO. Goes to 7 if K=1; goes to 1∅ if K=2, etc.
GO TO $i,(n_1,n_2, \ldots , n_m)$	GO TO K,(5,8)	Assigned GO TO. Goes to 5 if K=5; goes to 8 if K=8.
LOGICAL list	LOGICAL X,A	Variables listed are logical variables and are only TRUE or FALSE.

TABLE A-2 FORTRAN IV STATEMENTS NOT EXPLAINED IN TEXT

Statement	Example	Explanation
PAUSE	PAUSE	Causes computer to halt execution until instructions to proceed are received.
REWIND *n*	REWIND 6	Causes tape 6 to be rewound to beginning.

TABLE A-3 FORTRAN IV LIBRARY FUNCTIONS EXPLAINED IN TEXT

Function	Example	Section No.
absolute value (*a*)	ABS(X∗A)	6-3
ln (*a*)	ALOG(Z)	6-5
log (*a*)	ALOG1Ø(Y)	6-5
$\tan^{-1}$ (*a*)	ATAN(A/B)	6-7
cosine (*a*)	COS(BETA)[1]	6-6
e^a	EXP(X+A)	6-4
integer absolute value	IABS(K∗L)	6-3
sine (*a*)	SIN(A∗3.1416/18Ø.)[2]	6-6
$\sqrt{a}$	SQRT(X−A)	6-2
Also double precision forms of the preceding functions, that is, DSQRT(*A*), DEXP(*A*), etc.		11-4

[1] BETA expressed in radians.
[2] A expressed in degrees.

TABLE A-4 FORTRAN IV LIBRARY FUNCTIONS NOT EXPLAINED IN TEXT*

Function	Form	Function	Argument
Arc tangent	ATAN2(X,Y)	Real	Real
Choosing largest value	AMAXØ	Real	Integer
	AMAX1	Real	Real
	MAXØ	Integer	Integer
	MAX1	Integer	Real
	DMAX1	Real	Real
Choosing minimum value	AMINØ	Real	Integer
	AMIN1	Real	Real
	MINØ	Integer	Integer
	MIN1	Integer	Real
	DMIN1	Double	Double
Cosine	CCOS(U)	Complex	Complex
Exponential	CEXP(U)	Complex	Complex
Natural logarithm	CLOG(U)	Complex	Complex
Sine	CSIN(U)	Complex	Complex
Square root (complex)	CSQRT(U)	Complex	Complex

*Some FORTRAN packages may contain functions not listed in this table. It was felt these functions were so specialized in nature that it served no general purpose to include them. Students are reminded again always to check with the local computer center to find out what functions are available and how to use them.

APPENDIX B.

OPERATION OF THE IBM 029 CARD PUNCH

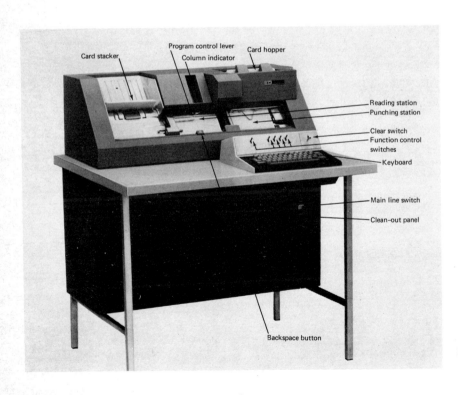

Card stacker • Program control lever • Column indicator • Card hopper • Reading station • Punching station • Clear switch • Function control switches • Keyboard • Main line switch • Clean-out panel • Backspace button

FIG. B-1
IBM 029 card punch. (*Courtesy of IBM.*)

A To prepare the card punch for operation:
1 Turn the *main line switch on.* (See Fig. B-1.) (This red-framed switch is located beneath the desk top at the upper right of the kick panel. To turn on, place the switch control in the "up" position.)

127

2 Place the first five (from left to right) *function control switches* in the "on" (up) position. (These switches are located on the control box just above the keyboard.) The toggle switch at the extreme right, marked CLEAR, is spring-loaded to remain in the "off" position.

3 Place the *program control lever* in the "off" position. (This butterfly-shaped lever is located just below and to the left of the column indicator at the center of the machine. The lever should be pushed *down* on the *right* side.)

4 Load the approproate blank cards (at least 25, 1/2 in. or more in thickness) in the *blank card hopper* (located in the top of the machine on the right side).

   a Release the pressure plate and push backward until it catches and remains back. (The plate has a catch lever located in the upper rear of the plate. Move the lever forward, and then the catch plate can be pushed backward.)

   b Place the appropriate cards in the hopper with the top of the cards up, printed face forward. Push to the front of the hopper, making sure the cards are all aligned and the top edges are even.

   c Release the pressure plate and slide it forward, pressing it firmly against the back of the stack of cards.

The card punch is now ready for the operator to begin punching.

B To punch only a few cards:

1 Depress the FEED key to bring a single blank card from the hopper into the punching station. (The FEED key is located on the right of the second row of keys from the top of the keyboard.)

2 Depress the REGister key to register the card so that column 1 of the card is aligned under the punching head. The *column indicator* should be aligned with the 1 graduation mark on the numbered drum. (The REGister key is just below the FEED key.)

3 The card is now ready to be punched with the appropriate alphanumeric characters in the desired columns.

   a Punch letters of the alphabet by depressing appropriate keys. The letter will also be printed at the top of the card.

   b Punch numerals or special characters by holding down the NUMERIC key and then depressing the appropriately marked key. The numeral or character will also be printed at the top of the card. (The NUMERIC key is the leftmost key in the bottom row of keys.)

   c Depressing the *space bar* will skip a card column without punching or printing. Holding the space bar down will skip one column at a time until the bar is released. Use of the space bar enables the operator to punch in the desired column, i.e., punching the FORTRAN statement starting in column 7. The number indicated on the column indicator is the *next* column to be punched (or skipped). (The space bar is the long bar beneath the bottom row of keys.)

   d Depressing the BACK SPACE button will move the card back one column at a time. Care should be taken to push this button *straight* *back.* Holding down the BACK SPACE button will repeat back spacing one column at a time until the button is released or until the card reaches column 1. The use of the space bar and the BACK SPACE button ensures that the operator can always align the desired card column under the punching head. (The BACK SPACE button is located off the keyboard to the left center of the reading station.)

4 When punching is completed on a given card, depress the RELease key. The punched card will move to the reading station, and a single blank card will be moved from the hopper to the punching station. (The RELease key is located just above the FEED key.)

5 Depress the REGister key to register the new blank card with column 1 under the punching head. The card is now ready for punching.

6 When the second card is punched, depressing the RELease key will cause the card that was in the reading station to move to the card stacker, move the just completed card to the reading station, and feed another blank card into the punching station.

7 When the last card is punched, pressing the CLEAR toggle switch upward will move all cards to the card stacker without feeding a new card to the punching station. Thus the card punch is cleared for the next operator. The cards in the card stacker will be arranged face up in the order punched.

C To punch a number of cards:

1 Depress the FEED key twice. The first blank card fed into the punching station will be registered, and a second blank card will be ready to be registered subsequently.

2 Since the first card is registered, the REGister key should *not* be depressed. Punching can now be done as described previously.

3 When the first card is punched, depressing the RELease key will move the first card to the reading station, register the card that was waiting in the punching station, and feed another blank card to the punching station to be registered subsequently.

4 When the last card is punched, pressing the CLEAR toggle switch upward will move all cards to the card stacker without feeding any cards into the punching station. It should be noted, however, that the last card in the card stacker will be a blank card which should be removed and saved for later use.

D To duplicate a punched card:

1 Insert the card to be duplicated into the empty reading station, carefully sliding it through the guides provided.

2 Insert a blank card in the empty punching station, again sliding it through the guides provided.

3 Depress the REGister key. This will align column 1 of both cards under the respective reading and punching heads.

4 Depress and hold down the DUPlicate key until all punching is completed. (The DUPlicate key is located in the top row of keys just above the Y and U keys.)

5 Pressing the CLEAR toggle switch upward will move both cards to the card stacker.

E If the keyboard is locked, depress the ERROR RESET key (located at the extreme left of the keyboard just above the NUMERIC key).

F When all punching is completed:
1 Press the CLEAR toggle switch upward to clear all cards from the punching and reading stations.
2 Remove all cards from the card stacker.
3 Remove all cards from the blank card hopper and replace in storage racks unless the next operator is waiting and desires those particular cards.
4 Place all discarded cards in the proper receptacle.
5 Turn off the main line switch unless the next operator is waiting for the machine.

INDEX